Stories on the timeline of man,
photographs and drawings
Erkki Luoma-aho, 2015

Translated by Vilma Lauhakangas

1. Run, take cover
65,000,000 years ago

Yucatán

A fireball with a diameter of fifteen kilometers crashes Earth at a horrendous speed, filling the air with fiery stones and ash. Within moments a shock wave destroys everything in the area throughout hundreds of kilometers.

Somewhere in Western Sahara

In a few days, the ash clouds and the clouds of gas that have spread to the atmosphere have turned the western sky purple. The Sun sets maybe for the last time before the never-ending night.

The necks of giant lizards stand out black against the sky as they dine on the savannah. They have no idea that this might be their last supper.

Grey ash falls on everything that is green. The air starts to cool. Nature becomes silent. Terror-stricken, the animals start to seek shelter.

A small group of proto-primates, creatures less than ten centimeters high, are frolicking on the rock. The males use finger-wrestling in a civilized manner to determine the leader of the harem. The leader orders the group to flee to a vast cave complex they have dug underground. The mouths of the cave are sealed up neatly, by using the thumb and the index finger. Even though primates are terrestrial animals, their true abilities are revealed when they escape predators using trees and lianas.

After a few days, the bravest proto-primates dare to step out and smell the air, but due to bitter smoke they are forced to retreat back to the caves. Their food supplies will do for now, but more has to be provided. At least they are not short of water yet: enough water oozes through the layers of sand. Sounds of birds and small mammals start to carry from outside. A new search reveals the awful truth, the scavengers fight over the corpses of dead dinosaurs and other large animals. The herbivores are weak because the ash and the acid rain have destroyed the flora. Due to the darkness there will be no growth. The beasts preying on the herbivores are also gone.

Only after three years the clouds of dust begin to vanish and the sunlight is able to reach the surface of the Earth. Small mammals take over the void created by the disappearance of the giant lizards. A new day dawns also to the proto-primates, but it will take tens of millions of years for the first apes and hominids to appear on Earth.

2. Over the smoldering ash
Laetoli, 3,600,000 years ago

At this hour of the day, the heat of the Sun is agonizingly hot. In the sky the sun appears in the shade of red ocher. The animals of the savannah feel the same agony. The gazelles are leaping over the plain, their hooves hardly touching the red ash as they bounce to another long leap.

The painful journey of the family of three continues endlessly over the searing landscape. Only the occasional areas of tussocks and small wetlands ease their pain. The father carries the small one over the worst parts. The ash rain still continues and the bigger lumps burn their skin to blisters.

It is vital to spend the night somewhere safe. Facing the large felines in an open savannah would bring their escape to an end. The path heads down a cliff towards the west. They have to find a hollow that can be closed for the night. Luckily down the slope there are fruit trees that can provide for them until the next morning.

- Look daddy, the sun is setting brightly.
- Tomorrow we head in the same direction!
- I'm hungry! Do we have water?

- Mom! It burns!
- Not there! Over here onto the grass.

There was a grassy savannah ahead. All the growth was gray with ash. The trees and bushes were spreading a bitter smoke.

3.   Robbers of fire
Koobi Fora, 1,600,000 years ago

The men of the village have taken their spears and are heading out for a hunting trip to a nearby canyon in a river valley. The darkness of the night turns to twilight and the Sun glistens over the mountain tops. The women stay to take care of the little ones. A couple of young men are left to protect the women and to help in the daily chores, including looking after the fire and guarding the water. They have agreed on guarding shifts and will alert the others in case of wild animals and intruders.

The most valuable treasure of the community is guarded by the eldest of the village. The eternal flame is buried under layers of rocks and sand. The elder softly throws sand over the eternal fire. The ability to store fire has remained in the community for decades, even centuries. Fire brings safety to the darkening nights, predators stay away and even the poisonous spiders and scorpions flinch at the light and flee to their holes. The nights spent by the fire bring the group closer to each other.

From up above the rocks, a herd of deer is spotted dining by the riverside. The hunting crew divides into two groups. The quickest get to be chasers while the strongest hide out between the river canyon's rocks, ready to strike their spears into the fleeing deer.

Two strangers manage to sneak into the camp. They watch the fire burn in awe. How could this be... The last fire given by the sky was months ago. Where did the fire come from? The question was directed at the elder who draws images to the sand with a piece of a burnt stick. Is it there? The strangers rush to the drawings and start to dig with their hands.
- Dig all you want - there's nothing there!

The deer hunt was a success and the hunters return to the camp with their kill and begin a cheerful tune.

- Aei o u o-o ouu, aei o u o-o ouu
Deer's bottom, deer's bottom
Wonderful, wonderful...
   The campfire is already in view. Memories of sizzling meat put a spring in their steps. Is everything alright? The people have all gathered by the eternal flame. On the ground, there are two men struggling in agony and asps are slithering to their pits. The sand has once again kept its secret.

4.   Disappearances
Atapuerca, 430,000 years ago

The sun has just risen from behind the mountains of Atapuerca, lighting up a small cavity in the rock that has been the home for a community for years. Actually it's rather comfy, the ledge protecting the community from rain and storms.

- We're in need of brave men to solve these strange disappearances. A week ago we lost five men who were hunting at a nearby gorge. No traces were left behind to explain how they disappeared. It was like the earth had swallowed them.

- Maybe the earth did swallow them! Rainwater has carved the entire hillside and there could be mountain lions living up there. Maybe there is a mouth of a bigger cave somewhere, hidden behind the bushes. I want to go on an expedition with you!

- Remember to keep enough distance between each other as there is a chance that there will be no one left to tell the story. Be sure to take your weapons with you, mountain lions are fierce when protecting their cubs.

Soon there is a group of six rallied up and heading towards the gorge. They climb up and down the hillside. In the afternoon, only a craggy area covered in shrubbery remains to be searched. It's starting to rain. The water carries mud making the rocks slippery.

- Hey, over here, I think I found something!

The group is standing around a black hole. The slippery rocks begin to tumble into the abyss and yet another expedition comes to an unlucky end.

5.   Beauty of the village
Tan-Tan, 400,000 years ago

- These rocks are sacred to us. The spirits of the mountains still live among us in their contours and shadows.

- That's true, but what is that rock that you're holding?

- It takes time before the spirits of the dead become boulders with human faces. I thought that I'd speed things up.

- How could that be done?

- The same way we use stones to make tools. I tried to carve shapes into the rock. This one already looked like it had a human figure. I thought I'd help nature a bit. Here is the beauty of our village!

- I wouldn't have guessed!

- A shapely figure is best suited for use as a model. You don't want to grind the waist too thin or the stone will break.

- Sorry, but is this the front or the back?

- Your knowledge of anatomy seems to be a bit tenuous. You can decide for yourself!

6. I went around the Sun
Bhimbekta, 300,000 years ago

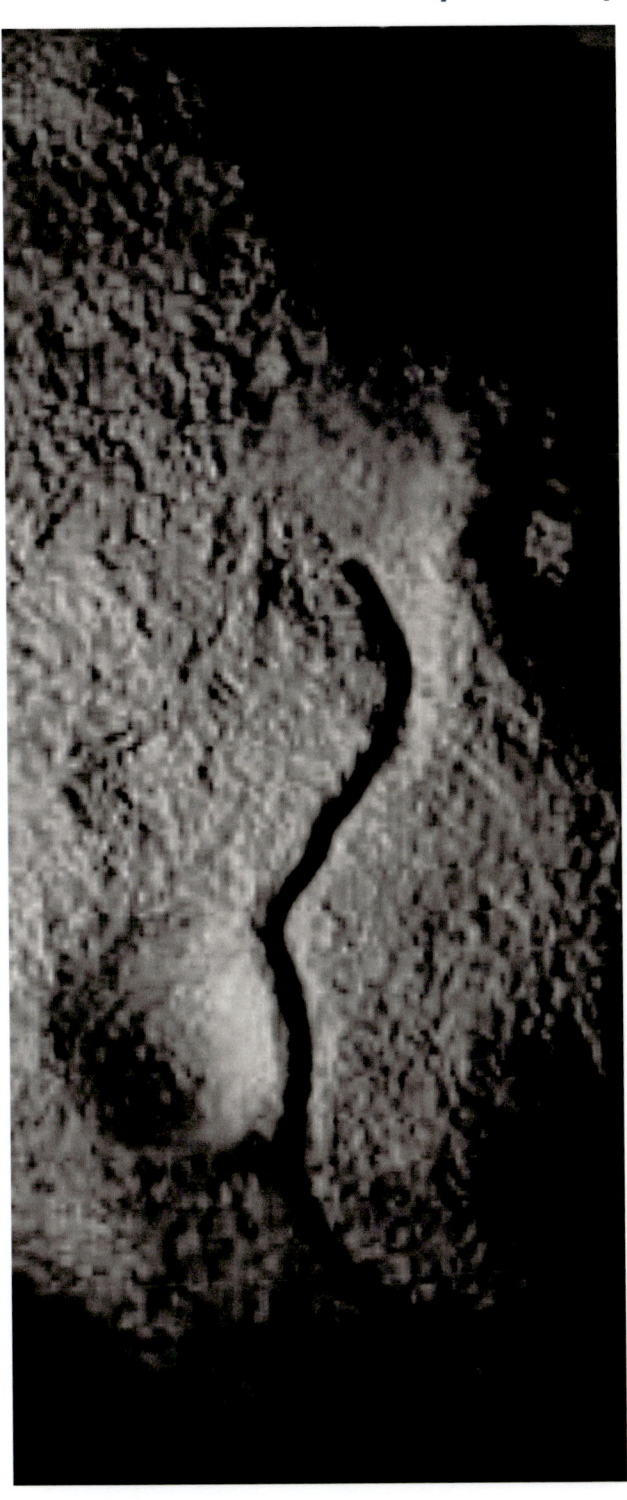

- I carved a picture into the rock about my journey!

- Where did you go?

- The Sun, well, almost. I rushed straight on to a sea of fire, went around the Sun a couple of times and then lifted the hem of my cloak and got slammed back by the solar winds.

- Quite supernatural that experience of yours.

- And that's not all. I've carved around ten stories about my journeys into the rock, just to show what isn't worth trying out. Will you look at that pile of skin! The surface of all of the skin clothing has been burned.

- Here's a quick analysis of your situation: Stop this madness at once or you could get hurt. Change your medication!

7. The skier and the bow
Wolf cave, 130,000 years ago

Karijoen Sanomat-newspaper
9/30/2014, EL

When the National Board of Antiquities stopped funding the excavations of the Wolf cave, a local amateur archeologist was free to do additional research in the cave. As he was removing a waste pile from a back corner, he found a new cavity that had gone unnoticed. The narrow cavity was two meters long and led to a room the size of a few square meters where one could easily move in an upright position. When the researcher stepped into the chamber the sight was breathtaking; the walls were painted with red ocher paint, resembling the finest painted caves in the Pyrenees.

- What was your first impression when you walked into the chamber?

- I have visited the Paleolithic caves of Spain and France several times, but everything was somehow more primitive here. Our view of the Neanderthals is about to change completely. The first paintings, made by the Neanderthals 43,000 years ago, were found in the Nerja caves in Spain. These must be nearly three times their age.

An interesting detail in the middle of the painting is a skier carrying a bow and next to him there are circles of a target board. About 140 km from here there is a big biathlon center under construction. What a weird coincidence!

- And the floor is filled up with the most wonderful stone tools. They are nothing like the simple items in the main cave!

New paintings of Wolf cave, DStretch processing EL

8.   Mixed messages
Asturia, 49,000 years ago

Each year winter arrives earlier to the Asturian Mountains. Snow has covered the scenery under its heavy blanket, making the steep slopes difficult to cross. A month ago, nearby in a crossing of two rivers, deer were being hunted for winter sustenance. Finding prey in a two-meter thick crust of snow during the early spring can be very difficult and many families struggle at the edge of starvation.

A fate worse than starvation could lie ahead. Hunger made some groups resort to desperate measures such as taking over shelters, murdering inhabitants and stealing the deer meat meant for winter. The inhabitants were also eaten before the group was forced to move on to the next target.

An alarm system was also set up for the deer hunting. Smoke signals were used to alert the neighborhood of possible threats, real danger or sometimes telling the people that there seemed to be no danger at all.

On the darkest day of the year, a smoke signal a mile away to the east is noticed, followed by a line of three signals. This means that the threat is extreme. The camp of El Sidrón is also preparing for the worst. After a while, a message arrives that brings relief to the camp; two signs- the situation has calmed down and life gets back to normal.

The camp is closely guarded. Two months have passed and there is no sign of the group that made the alarm. Black Hat decides to go and investigate the situation. The spring sun has melted the snowy slope and it has hardened again during the night freeze. Black Hat is able to walk upon the snow. He leaves at dawn. The laborious route goes through a river that is partly frozen. In a few hours Black Hat reaches the campsite. The inhabitants of the rock shelter seem to be awake and outside. He doesn't recognize anybody. Strangers have taken over the campsite.

There's no time to waste as he begins his exhausting journey back. When he arrives home, he informs others of the situation in the neighboring cave. Precautions are taken immediately. The families living in the west have to be warned. Despite the risk of exposure, a fire has to be lit. To save time, Black Hat plans to send the signal of great danger, three smoke signs. He manages to send two before he collapses by the fire, pierced by a sharp arrow...In the neighboring shelter the inhabitants cheer for the time of peace. All is well in the east...
 Spring arrives at the hills of El Sidrón and the two-meter high snow banks melt rapidly turning into streams and

rapids. They run underground, disappearing, and carving the cave system. The raiders who took over the cave have moved westward. The change in the terrain is visible: solid rocks have disappeared to the ends of the earth, carried by the stream of water. The same thing happens to the rock shelter of El Sidrón. Within moments it sinks deep into the water, taking with it the evidence of brutal murders and scraped bones.

9. In the light of the seal fat lamp
Nerja, 42,000 years ago

- Raise that oil lamp of yours a little bit higher! I'm trying to climb up there to finish my seal-painting. It was left unfinished when I didn't dare to go up the ladder with the lamp and colors. The lamp I left burning on the ground didn't give enough light and my body was blocking what little it did give.

- Is this OK? Seals are the most important prey animals. Unfortunately we were able to kill them only during their mating season. I heard from the hunters that they've tried using fishnets for sealing. First it was by accident when some seals got caught in the nets and tore them up. Now they're working on a newer and stronger model that could enable the seals being pulled up.

- For my work the seal fat is more important than its meat. There are enough deer and other wild animals in the woods, and seal meat isn't really to my liking. But without light I can't manage in the cave and it is rather nice to be able to see in the cave after sundown. The seal fat lamp illuminates longer than a campfire where you continuously need to add wood to the fire. Not to mention the wood has to be carried from a greater and greater distance away.

- Where did you get the idea of painting pictures on the pillars of the dripstone cave?

- I happened to try mixing red ocher with grease and blood. The color does stay on the rock but it didn't stick on the rock shore. The rains and the sea waves washed it away in seconds. You must recognize the red ocher from the funeral rituals. I have the same holiness now in my pictures. Let's hope these paintings strengthen our fortune in hunting and make the seals come rushing to the shore.

10. This is mine
Leang Timpuseng, 40,000 years ago

- This hog deer is mine! The whole rock is mine!

- No one owns nature, it belongs to everyone!

- Take a look at my palm print a little left from the hog deer. It's my mark of ownership.

- Be careful with what you're doing. Soon all the palefaces will do the same, saying they own this and that, trading and imposing taxes on things. It will only lead to disagreements and war! Grow up and wash that slurry of lime off your face!

11. Finger bone
The Cave of Denisova, 40,000 ya

- Here's another bucket of stuff from the bottom of the cave. I also removed some objects. There was a small piece of bone, maybe from a bird or a small mammal. But we have enough of those.

- Come now, don't belittle our findings. All bones must be collected. They can be used to make datings. In this way we can find out the chronology of the different layers that we are analyzing.

- Well, everything we dig up goes down the rope line. Our archeologists go through all the material one more time. If nothing interesting is found, everything goes to a huge waste pile.

On March 2010, there was an announcement that the remains of a Denisovan hominin had been found from the Ayu-Tash Cave in Altai. The cave is also known as the Denisova Cave, named after the hermit Dionisij (Denis) who lived there. A small piece of finger bone reshaped our understanding of human prehistory. DNA studies showed this human species lived side by side with the Neanderthals, and has close relatives in modern Southeast Asia. Research shows that the people with the largest share of Denisonovan-derived DNA in their genome are Papua New Guineans. Later excavations yielded a tooth and a toe bone.

12. Bulls on the ceiling
Altamira, 35,000 years ago

Don Marcelino Sanz de Sautuola (1831-88) is usually considered to be the one who discovered the bull paintings of Altamira, but in fact it was his five year old daughter who made the discovery.

Don Marcelino had taken his daughter with him to the cave like many times before. She got bored while watching her father do his excavations.

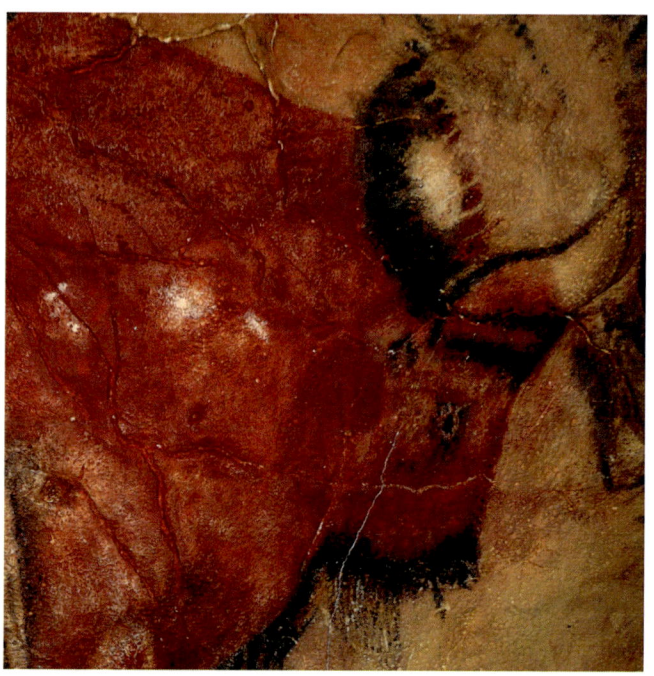

To pass the time, she moved the candle light towards the bumpy ceiling. All of a sudden she exclaimed: "Toros, toros!" meaning "bulls, bulls" in Spanish.

"Did you say you see bulls? Where do you see them?"

"There!" exclaimed Maria, pointing to the red images.

"They are just shadows, nothing to be afraid of! The light is creating illusions."

"No, no, there are many bulls and they're all red!"

Don Marcelino wiped the dirt off his hands and touched her little daughter's forehead. "We have to go home. You have a cold and you might have a fever." Realizing the girl's forehead was cool, Don Marcelino shook his head puzzled. He got down on his

knees and leaned back to view the ceiling but didn't see anything. It was only after Maria pointed at the red bull with a pickaxe, that Don Marcelino was able to make out its four hooves and large eye. In the candle light, it looked as if the animal was stirring and still breathing.

Thus was found the first Paleolithic cave decorated with paintings (1879).
  Summary from the book "The Caves of the Great Hunters" by Hans Baumann (WSOY, 1957)

13. Human-like
The Cave of Apollo 11, 30,000 ya

A team led by a German archeologist Wolfgang Wendt found red paintings in the Cave of Goachanas in Southern Namibia representing geometric figures and at least one unidentified animal. They were painted on seven quartzite plates.

July 24th of 1969

- The name the locals have given the cave is pretty simple. We should give it a new name. It is a significant finding. Any suggestions?

- How about The Cave of Apollo 11? The astronauts have safely landed on Earth as we heard on the radio.

- Proposition accepted. A splendid name and the time of the event will surely be remembered!

- This has been divided into two plates. What do you think it represents? I think there's some smooth and cat-like movement in it.

- Look at those hind legs, they're clearly human!

14. The cave lions
Chauvet, 30,000 years ago

- Dear friends! We should decide on what actions to take regarding the cave lions. With all due respect to the magnificent felines, we do not fit in the same cave system. Any suggestions?

- We'll build a stone wall in front of the main entrance, including the cavities that lead to the cave system. If the lions cannot get out it will only be a matter of time when they start attacking each other.

- That's a horrible end for such noble animals! Besides, we don't know of every underground passage leading outside. I propose we set a big fire inside the cave. The smoke will surely force the cats out.

- Both are good suggestions, maybe we'll combine the two. We can take logs and tree branches into the cave and use torches to protect ourselves and to light the fire. We should be prepared to close the main entrance quickly. The smoke should then reveal the rest of the underground passages.

- The spears of our hunters can protect us, but we don't want a mass slaughter and I'm sure the beasts will run away from the fire and smoke. Then we'll just block the entry ways and our future in the cave system will be secured!

15. Bent fingers
Cosquer, 27,000 years ago

A French diver called Henri Cosquer found this cave in 1985. The mouth of the cave is now 37 meters below sea level. Leading to the cave is an underwater tunnel which is 175 meters in length. The discovery was announced in 1991 when three divers got lost and drowned in the cave system.

During the Ice Age the sea level was approximately 120 meters lower than today. It is estimated that 3 out of 4 of the rock paintings were destroyed when the water level rose.

There are about 200 pictures of animals in the cave. The paintings and carvings represent 11 different breeds including horses, bisons, aurochs, red deer, alpine goats (chamois, ibexes), deer, antelopes and felines. There are also sea animals such as seals, fish, razorbills, jellyfish, penguins and squid, and an anthropomorph that has a human body, but the head of a seal.

There are also 44 black and 21 red palm prints in the cave and over 200 different geometric figures. The palm paintings are imperfect: many of the fingers seem to be cut off. The same observation has been made in similar caves.

The researchers believe that because the finger bones found from that period of time are not broken, the imprints were made with bent fingers. It might represent sign language of sorts, but its meaning is not known.

16. Let me scream
Brassempouy, 23,000 years ago

A Venus sculpture (size 3.65 x 1.9 x 2.2cm) with a human face was found from the Cave of Bressempouy in Southwest France in 1892. The figurine representing a beautiful woman is made from ivory and her hair is reminiscent of Ancient Egyptian style.

What makes the figurine special is that even though the eyes and nose are clean-cut, her mouth is missing. We do not know whether this has something to do with the personality of the model or if it is a tradition.

- I see you're all dolled up!
I thought that this time we would only make a portrait of your face. The material I've chosen is ivory. I think it reflects best the lightness of your skin.

We can try to make a full-body model later, but it takes more time.

- I don't know yet, if I want to reveal so much of myself!

- Yes, I can see that you are carrying a secret inside you. May I ask who the happy father is?

- No, you may not. Since you asked my answer is simply: I won't tell you!

- Fine, suit yourself. May the portrait only tell what you want it to!

17. Where did the dog go?
Lascaux, 20,000 years ago

One of the valleys of Lake Dordogne in the south of France had a strange incident on the 12th of August 1940. Four boys were walking on the south side of Montignac through an oak grove when suddenly a dog that was with them disappeared. While the boys were looking for it, they found a cave on the hill of Lascaux and saw that its walls were full of pictures of animals: horses, elk, ibexes and aurochs.

When they told their teacher about the incredible discovery, he was over the moon and started to dance wildly. After he calmed down, he alerted a well-known researcher called Abbott Breuil to come from Paris to see the discovery.

From "The Caves of the Great Hunters" by Hans Baumann (WSOY, 1957)

18. Boomerang throwers
Burrup, 20,000 years ago

Welcome to Boomerang School!

Today we will learn how the boomerang is used as a weapon for battle and hunting. In this picture, the young men are practicing with boomerangs as big as themselves. It's clear that these are not used for throwing. With these, you take a good grip with two hands and strike down an animal or your enemy from a close distance.

With a boomerang the size of your arm, your prey can be hit from a few dozen steps away. You throw straight at the animal that can be on the ground or in a tree.

This here is our latest model which can be used for catching flying birds. The best part is that if you miss, the boomerang flies back to your hand! It works best when you use it headwind.

It's almost as if the boomerang has wings when it goes around the prey and catches it by surprise. It takes time to learn how to throw it but after you do, you don't have to go searching for the weapon every time you use it.

For the best result, we have combined the use of the bird net with the boomerang. A flock of birds can be steered to the right direction with a skillful throw.

We are now really focusing on this great gadget. These here are half-finished and now we can start to improve their ability to fly. You can review the model piece to find out where and in what direction you have to thin it out. Notice that if you're left-handed you have to think of it like a mirror-image.

When we move on to the practice of throwing, some caution is required; you don't want to be loitering in the direction others are throwing. The boomerang is fast and its sharp edges can easily reshape your heads or bodies!

Good luck working with your boomerang!

19. The most touching image
Abri de la Madeleine, 20,000 ya

- Have you heard of the Junior Picture Competition? The theme is nature and you can take part with paintings, drawings, sculptures and even poems. You're given a week to finish your work and the winners are announced in the Spring Festival of the Equinox.

- I thought of participating. I have deer's horn and some sharp pieces of flint. I'm going to observe bisons at the shore meadow, would you like to join me?

The two friends return to the river bank several times to finish their pictures.

- My work is finished. Do you think I could also write a poem about it?

People have gathered at the spring festival and everyone is waiting to see who will be chosen as this year's Junior Artist.

- The most touching image of nature is.... "A bison licking a mosquito bite". Artist, come and present your work!

"Bison, you boasting bovine,
come here with those scars of yours.
All the other bulls you won
but to the small mosquito you could do none!"

20. Does my hair look OK?
Serra da Capivara, 20,000 ya

About 780 km northwest from the town of Salvador, in the National Park of Sierra da Capivara in Brazil, lies the oldest known human settlement in South America. People lived here already 50,000 years ago.

The oldest rock paintings and drawings originate from almost the same period and the oldest datings are from 26,000-22,000 years ago.

The images on the rock tell a rich story about life in the area: people hunting and performing ritual-like dances. Wildlife presented in the pictures include giant sloths, horses and llamas. Bones of ocelots, bush dogs and saber-toothed tigers have also been found.

The picture above is typical to the area, but we cannot be sure what is going on in it. There's a line of men with decorations in their hair, women are on their knees holding their hands up and there are also people in crooked positions. Are the latter ones dead? Is this a funeral procession?

21. Deep carvings
Winnemucca, 15,000 years ago

- Deep carvings!

- Yes, carved deep into the rock and into our hearts. I'm making the lines even more deep. We have to cherish the memory of our ancestors. Everywhere you look you can see we treasure nature.

- I've heard the Eastern tribes carve stick-figures to the rocks. That's not our thing is it?

- No, it's not. The generations from the past talk to us through the Sun and the storm clouds which strike down if we've done something wrong. The woods protect us. The waves roar or sometimes whisper to us in soft breezes. My favorite picture is the one with the honeycombs, the honeybees are our friends.

- But where are the animals? We don't live on plants alone.

- We do have a hunting gallery. It's on the other side of the lake where there is rough terrain. It is open for dedicated hunters only.

- Our past has started to interest me. Are we originally from the North as so many presume?

- I'd say our roots are in the South. After dozens of generations, we still haven't gotten used to this cold breeze...

22. The Gallery of the Ancient Animals
Kapova, 15,000 years ago

- Here you are, our favorite painter. I tried to enter from above, but the cave's entrance is blocked. It must have been an earthquake that caused the ceiling to collapse. I had to enter from below which wasn't easy because the river seems to be flooding again. I had to wade through the cold water and my fire went out when I slipped on the rocks. Luckily I remembered the route. Can I come and warm myself by your fire?

- Please come in. The cave collapsing was actually my own doing. I was frightened terribly when I heard a saber-tooth right behind me, but luckily I was able to snatch a fiery ember and chase it away. I didn't want to be caught off guard anymore. I managed to move the flagstone and add smaller stones to seal the entrance tight.

- You sealed it nice and tight, but the saber-tooth story sounds silly. No one has seen them for a while, they disappeared right about the time the mammoths did. The saber-tooth used to chase baby mammoths.

- I guess there are no woolly rhinos here either. Maybe my collection should be named as "The Gallery of the Ancient Animals".

- Come now, we just ran into a herd of horses when we were scouting. A shift in prey is happening and our council is looking into it. There's no point in a hunting quota if the animals are moving to greener pastures.

- A horse steak is fine if there's nothing better available. Did you visit other villages on your expedition? What's new in the Ural Mountains?

- Yes, we did visit and speaking of horses we heard a story about a man who had tried to travel on a horse's back. Of course, it didn't work and he fell flat on his face and died instantly.

- Did he get a chance to tell why he would do such a thing?

- Not really. The last thing he said was: "Just wait until I tame you!"

23. Rhinoceros
Wadi Mathkendush, 12,000 ya

- So they put us to a hunting test as if we didn't have enough merits! What should we hunt? It has to be big, fast and mean!

- How about a lion? A lion hunter is respected. Although, if you miss a shot, it could be your last. Even the fastest of legs won't help.

- We'll catch a rhino!

- That might be too big of a challenge. A rhino's feet have trampled dozens of hunters. I doubt our spears will pierce its armor.

- Yes, it's big, fast and powerful, but it's also stupid and blind. I've got a plan.

They took a tall and heavy spear and sharpened one end. They then dug the other end to the sand until the spearhead was about a meter above ground. The two men positioned themselves in front of the spear and started to aggravate a nearby rhino by making feint attacks. The animal charged the men...

- Let's stay still as long as we can. I'll shout when it's time to move aside.

Will the two men disturbing the dining rhino get trampled as many have before them?
This time the trick worked and the rhinoceros rushed straight towards the spear, into certain death.

- Where did you come up with this clever scheme?

- Everything is based on the fact that rhinos have poor vision. This deficiency makes them quick to anger and that's when you need to keep your wits about you. I went with the advice of an experienced hunter when he was asked what he does when a rhino attacks, he answered: nothing. I just quietly wait until the last minute and then rush out of the way. The rhinoceros will keep going for about a hundred meters. What if it attacks again?
I do the same all over again, it'll tire after a few times!

- Let's put on our fox masks to show how clever we are. We still have to complete the slog of hauling our catch to the rest of the tribe!

24. The tooth of a dog
Pulli, 11,000 years ago

The spring migration to the mouth of the river is about to start. The dugouts have been loaded and the additional baggage is placed on the rafts tied with willow bast.

Rover is eager for the journey to start. It is standing proudly in the first dugout with its paws on the edge of the bow.

Many times has Rover saved its masters from food bandits, whether they were people, bears or other creatures of the forest.

The journey to the Big Lake usually takes a day or two depending on the ordeals faced on the journey. This time the journey took only a day. Winter is gone and the light of the day lasts longer. A campfire is still needed.

A summer village is being built at the river's mouth. The population has grown and new huts are needed. They are being constructed from slates and dead trees.

Tomorrow the bast nets have to be taken near the rushes where the fish are. The migratory birds have also arrived. Nesting birds are not usually hunted, but a few birds might still end up on the breakfast plates.

The routines established over the years and decades guide the daily activities. In the fall, the cold sea breeze forces the villagers to pull back into the woods by the upper stream.

In 1967, the remains of human settlements and animal bones were found from Pulli in Southwestern Estonia. A single dog's tooth revealed that dogs have been a part of the human communities for at least 11,000 years.

25. The Duel
Wadi Mathkendush, 11,000 ya

Goliath, a duelist from Ghat, located behind the Acacus Mountains, stepped out from the enemy camp. At 12 foot and a half, he was a giant.

"Choose a man amongst you to fight against me. If I win, you shall be our slaves. If I lose, you shall determine our destiny".

Fearless David stepped forward and picked five tree branches from the river bank. He faced the invincible Goliath who was riding a huge elephant.

"Do I look like a dog who wants a stick? Come here and I'll feed your flesh to the birds and the beasts!"

David threw a spiky branch at the eyes of the elephant and banged the sticks together making a horrible noise. The elephant stampeded and stumbled, causing Goliath to fall and plunge head-on to the rock. Goliath's troops fled to the mountains of Acacus.

This is the story of how little David beat the giant Goliath. He returned to Mathkendush in triumph.

26. The Baker of Sefar
Tassili n'Ajjer, 10,000 years ago

A black woman is standing in her kitchen corner next to a flagstone. On the table there are wild oat seeds gathered from the savannah. She is grinding the seeds with a polished, crescent-shaped tool. Delighted about her new job as the baker of the village, she is dressed in her finest. Wearing a cloak on her hips, pearls on her neck and a mask on her face she is performing the holy ritual of baking the bread.

In her mind, she goes through the instructions given to her by her grandmother:

One part flour
One quart of fat
One quart of milk
One eighth of herbs
One eighth of termites
One eighth of honey
A pinch of salt

The ingredients are mixed and the dough is placed on the baking stone. The bread sits there in the sun two to three hours until it's ready for eating.

The artist of the village arrives at the kitchen corner with his palette.

- Hello, can you spare a slice of that fat for me? It's good for binding the colors.
- Sure, I can leave you some.
- Good, now that the bread is baking, we can move to another spot. We must immortalize the village baker! Here is a good spot. That crack shall be the table where the seeds are crushed.

The artist is mesmerized by his own work.

- Should we add a date? Oh well, something for the next generations to ponder on...

27. The Solar Calendar
Magura, 10,000 years ago

- I got an assignment from the Chief to paint a solar calendar on the cave wall. It should mark the most important events of the year that have to do with hunting and fishing, and also the festivals.

- That's great! Something for the young ones to learn and to strengthen the memory of the old ones.

- Right now the problem is that the land is dry and there's no ocher, only limestone.

- Don't worry, have you tried that black goo on the cave's floor?

- No, it smells disgusting. What is it?

- It's the vampire's "you know what" and there's plenty of it. You could paint the walls and the ceiling if you wanted to.

- I could try if it sticks to the limestone. We will need adhesive, blood and grease.

- I might have a solution for your problem. Here is the blood of a real human vampire. Just days ago we were celebrating our liberation from the creature.

- I wasn't there, tell me everything.

- We drove the monster to a corner in its castle and carried out the actions we were told to do. We cut off its head and pushed a sharp stake through the heart. I dripped some of the blood to a bowl without really thinking about it. It sure was scary-looking with its red hair and only one huge nostril.

- Are you sure you didn't think about drinking the blood and turning into a vampire yourself? I have to monitor your behavior!

- That didn't cross my mind. I brought this to you, so you can paint your pictures.

- I'm a little worried about using it in the painting. Aren't vampires shape-shifters? What if it regenerates itself from the blood? If that happens and I'm found guilty, my life's worth nothing.

- I doubt that will happen. The heavy wooden stake lasts longer than the corpse. Think of it as an homage to all the young girls it drained the life of. They will have eternal life in your painting.

28. Revenge of the Sea-monster
Antrea, 10,000 years ago

Thicket twigs are good for nets,
willow bast bends to beckets,
bits of pine bark makes it float,
hidden rocks to make it hold.

Two fine fishermen,
launched their boat afloat.
Ahti, give us all your perch,
Wellamo will have her gold.

Sea-monster, the Gaffer's son
diving in the stream,
remembering the summer,
how he lost a brother.

What goes above the water?
Black shadow, casted net?
For perch they made this trap,
for pike they set this web.

The beast takes the stone,
and plunges to the abyss.
Edge pressed by the thread,
the dugout falls to depth.

The net fills up with rascals,
into the deeps of sea.
The message of the years past: the
revenge of the beast.

Erkki Luoma-aho, 2015

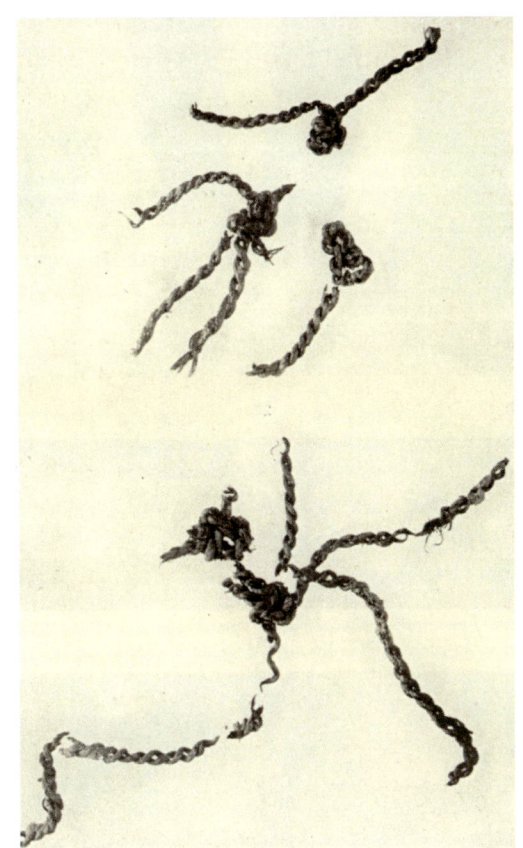

29. Time to dance
Tan Zoumaitak, 10,000 years ago

Travel log
Tan Zoumaitak, 11/9/2009

The enigmatic pictures of the round-headed people continue in the magnificent rock face of Tan Zoumaitak. The slender dancers with painted bodies, hair ornaments and bracelets fill up the upper part of the fresco. Most view the dancers as women although many researchers find them to be young men.

The dark images of the long-horned mouflons and the antropomorphs drawn in red complete the wall's splendor. There are also paintings with parts of different animals put together.

The shaman's little helper girl is playing a drum that has fringes. It's time for a rain dance!

30. The Hunters
Tin Tazarift, 10,000 years ago

- Well, this is a dreamlike picture. What's happening in it?

- Indeed, it is a dream. Our headmaster gave me this topic. It's a part of the glorious culture of the round-headed people.

- Why are we called roundheads?

- It's a sort of a contemptuous word. But we're going strong. Our faces are round because we have plenty of prey. The double arch in our bow is the foundation of our force!

- I sense some sadness in your picture. Didn't everything go according to plan?

- Everything was organized and the rabbit mask was on. When our Great Hunter was taking a new arrow from his quiver, he knew what was going to happen: the cave lion would win. From a distance, he saw a small antelope he wanted to give his soul to. The prey thus became his soulmate. They are united by the same enemy. In the picture, the antelope is taking in the hunter's strength. There's another hunter witnessing the incident and his life is also taken in this misfortune.

- And these characters on the left?

- They are our bullies, scampering away with their useless and old-fashioned weapons...

31. The Tree God
Šigir, 9,500 years ago

Travel log

8/2/2005, the Archaeological Museum of Yekaterinburg, Ural

We start to explore the ancient Ural at the Department of Archeology in the University of Yekaterinburg and later continue to the Archaeological Museum.

The findings from the swamp area of Šigir from the beginning of 1900s, are presented well. In the center, there is a Šigir idol over 5.5 meters high and some researchers say it is 9,500 years old. Its eyebrows, nose and round mouth are depicted in an intense fashion. The long body is combined from several parts with different ornaments: horizontal lines and diagonal zigzag lines.

It should be mentioned that a similar wooden image of a head has been found in Pohjankuru. The "Wooden God" is about 25 cm in height and has been dated to the Littorina Sea phase of the Baltic Sea. The head is presumed to be a part of a bigger whole, probably the head of a pillar.

Wooden God of Pohjankuru

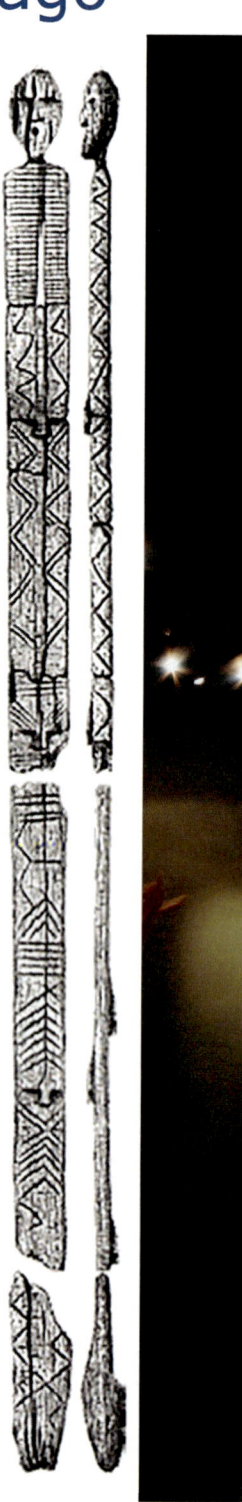

32. A dangerous mission
Nabta Playa, 9000 years ago

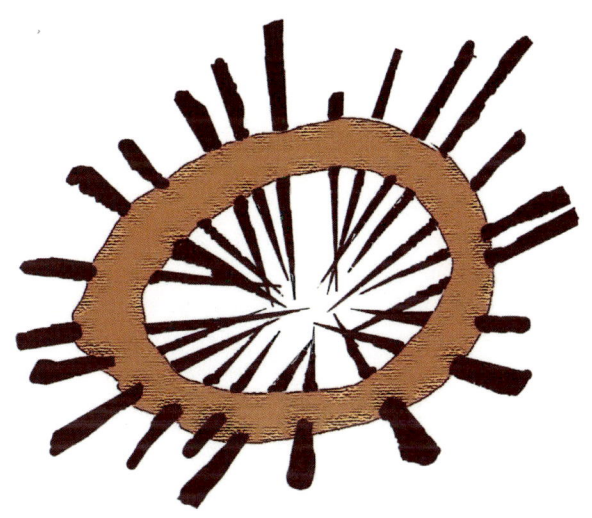

There is dry grass savannah as far as the eye can see. There are small lakes scattered where the grass is greener. Bushes and acacia trees also grow here, providing shade for the animals of the savannah.

Lion Ear and Lion Eye have received a mission pertaining to the rite of adulthood: they will have to catch a full-grown aurochs.

The boys are fully aware of how dangerous the task is even for adults. But they take it seriously and have equipped themselves with ropes and traps before heading off to the marshland where the aurochs usually dine. When the bulls are resting, the boys take a couple of traps consisting of sharp sticks and stone weights to a path that the bulls use and cover them carefully. Then they just wait with the ropes.

This devil of a trap is usually used to catch rhinos and giraffes. Although the aurochs is smaller than these animals, it is a force to be reckoned with. As the animal will have to be captured with as little harm as possible, they must quickly bind it with the ropes. Then the terrible traps can be removed and they can fetch help for the transporting of the bull.

33. On the broom
Ulldecona, 9000 years ago

- Looks like the one with the antlers got caught by surprise.

- Yeah. It must have been wondering what's whistling up above. The hunter got real close. It only took one arrow.

- You don't run out of tricks. Where did you get that thing?

- Usually, I go elk hunting with my familiar spirits but this time they refused. Of course, one day off per week is part of the contract. On the other hand, it was good to check on the old ride.

- Seems to be running OK. What maintenance procedures did you take?

- I changed a few tail twigs that were out of line. It's important that the steering is correct. Us witches gather to race on Walpurgis Night. We compete in speed, accuracy and stamina. If only someone would think of a way to tank up, there's plenty of room for a drinking bucket on the broom...

34. The Giraffe
Dabous, 9,000 years ago

Life-size drawings of giraffes astonish in the Aïr Mountains of Niger. They were carved into the sandstone 8,000 to 10,000 years ago.

All in all there are 828 drawings in the area: 704 pictures of animals (bovines, giraffes, ostriches, lions, rhinos and camels), 61 pictures of humans and 159 thus far unidentified subjects.

The largest giraffe is measured to be 5.40 m tall and 6.35 m wide. The line depth of the pictures is approximately 2 to 3 cm.

There are dangling lines leading from the mouths of the giraffes to the human figures. This might indicate that a man had attempted to tame the animals or they tell us a story about a symbolic relationship between the giraffe and man.
  Unfortunately, these pictures have also been vandalized. Visitors leave their own markings or even remove parts of the drawing and take them as souvenirs. Their shoes alone leave marks on the soft sandstone.

35. The Murder Mystery of Seraf
Tassili n'Ajjer, 8,000 years ago

Sahara Rock Art News (7/23/2014)

During his trip to Tassili n'Ajjer a Finnish rock art researcher made a peculiar discovery that might reveal events from 8,000 years ago.

He found an intact pot from the immediate distance of the Sefar cave paintings. When he poured the sand out of the vessel, there were seven stone arrowheads and bone chips at the bottom.

Were they bones from a hunted animal? Why were the arrowheads and bones in the same pot? While the researcher was pondering the issue he looked at a painting of a hunter with a drawn bow.

Beneath the hunter was an array of prey animals. This is the way the painting has been interpreted, but could they instead be human corpses? Chills went through the researcher when he noticed that there were seven dead figures.

He remembered reading that the French researcher and documenter of rock art Henry Lhote, mentions in his memoirs a skeleton found near the very same painting. The skeleton is now kept in the museum of Djanet.

The skeleton in the museum has a hole in its skull, apparently caused by one of the arrows that were found at the bottom of the pot.

The bone fragments from the pot turned out to be human right-hand index fingers. DNA from the finger bones is being processed. The first step will be finding out if it is the same as in the Djanet skeleton.

Excavations for finding the other six remaining victims are taking place. With the help of DNA, it might be possible to track the current relatives of the murdered victims.

36. Milk, milk!
Jebel Uweinat, 8,000 years ago

- What a pretty picture!

- I know, there's not always a clean stone cup for the twins and they've gotten too big for breast-feeding. In a way, it's easier that they get the milk straight from the cow. You don't have to wash the dishes all the time and get water from afar.

- Seems the cattle is used to living in captivity. Do you still remember the times when we were always on the move and following the prey animals? Nowadays it's different, we get milk and meat whenever we want.

- Now we can focus on new things. We must invest on sustainable living conditions. No one settles for a twig hut anymore. The cattle also needs a firm shelter because of the wild beasts.

- What are the men doing now, as hunting doesn't take up all of their time?

- They seem to be enjoying themselves in the pub downtown. Looks like a new batch of beer has been brewed...

- By the way, would you like to try out my new milk-based cake recipe?

37. Everything flows
Tamrit, 8,000 years ago

Travel log
Tamrit, Tassili n'Ajjer, 11/9/2009

Our 200 km journey in Tassili is coming to an end. The last location is in Tamrit which among other things has pictures of hunting.

Our eyes catch the spotted oblong images. What are they? A fish school, a pack of deer... The scale is confusing and none of the spots have any details that might help with the identification.

I decide to investigate a small cavity less than a meter high. I look to the top as I'm lying down on my back. I'm astounded when I notice that an area of one square-meter on the ceiling is covered with spotted illustrations that seem to be running in all directions. Light is scarce.

Camera settings: ISO-800, f/5, focal length 24mm, t=1/25 s.

I may have found a new cave painting in Tamrit, given that the pictures in the small cavity leave our guides clueless. As I work with DStretch-program at home, the patterns start to slightly resemble human figures. Pointillism from the Stone Age? Or are the pictures created by fungus gnat worms?
(EL)

38. East from the Nile
Wadi Hammamat, 8,000 years ago

Travel log
Wadi Hammamat, 12/15/2009

The purpose of the quick trip to Luxor was to see the rock art found between the Nile and the Red Sea in the Eastern Desert. The paintings nearest to Luxor were 150 km away in Wadi Hammamat.

I had previously acquired a permit to visit the Finnish excavations in the so-called Valley of the Kings. While I was asking travel agencies about traveling to the Eastern Desert I discovered that I would need a permission to get there. The paperwork would take a few days as the permit could only be picked up from Cairo and a police escort was also required.

After persistent negotiations, the travel agency agreed to give me the phone number of an archeologist guide. I contacted him and we arranged the trip. We left Luxor at dawn and drove to the desert avoiding the checkpoints on the way to Wadi Hammamat. In addition to the Stone Age pictures, there were also later productions and work that could be traced to the time of the Pharaohs.

As a thank you for a job well done, I arranged for a short trip to Abu Simbel and the temples by the Nile, between Luxor and Assuan.

39. Suursuo
Helsinki, 8,000 ya

I was approaching Suursuo. I slowed down and stopped to listen to the sounds of nature. I had been following the elks for a while. By looking at the tracks I could see their weary hooves had sunk deep into the snow.

On the edge of a marshland was a grassy area where the animals used to dine. I tried to peer through the branches and at first did not notice the small calf that was eating on its own. I slowly took out the bow from my back and reached for my finest arrows. The animal suddenly flinched and lifted its head. It had heard a wolf howling to its pack. The calf continued eating, but it was now much more alert and ready to move in a blink. I felt my heart racing thinking about the chase to come. It was a good thing the wolves were behind me because the calf would now have to run towards the marshland. The snow on the swamp carried a skier well but not a frightened elk.

I had heard many stories about elk skiing. Sometimes the hard snow crust would cut through the elk's skin revealing its shinbones when it was trying to escape from its hunter who had no trouble sliding on the snow wearing skis. The chase ended with the exhausted animal waiting for the final blow at the end of a bloody trail.

This was all new to me. I usually hunted rabbits using snares and I had a reputation as a skilled catcher of grouse.

It was my first time alone at Suursuo.

Before this, we had gathered moss and berries at the edge of the marshland. Cloudberry was my favorite and in winter the frozen berries brought back memories of summer. My carefree summers were over now since this year I was going to take part in the tribal activities which meant privileges but also responsibilities. This required passing the ordeal of the ritual with honor. But this was not the time to think of the future, this was the time to act.

The calf flinched again when two willow grouses flapped nearby, but kept eating. Six moons ago I had been on the same marshland but on the western end where there is usually much more game. We had only been watching a pack of elks without trying to hunt them. I had thought it strange but at the same time I understood that it was not right to hunt the mothers and their small calves. It was best to let them grow big and strong so they could survive in the harsh nature.

There was another reason: storing meat during summer was hard and nature had other things to offer for food.

Men and elks live in harmony during the summer. That is the way it shall always be. As if wanting to add weight to his word my father moved closer to a doe and its calf. I went behind him and the doe moved closer to its calf, but did not try to escape. I ripped a big tuft of grass from the ground and reached out to the small one. Slowly the calf came closer and gently took the grass off my hand. For a second, I felt its warm breath and looked into its big eyes. It had a unique mark below its left eye: a white spot. I named it Spot Eye.

After that, the elks gracefully joined the others on the marshland.

This was the first time my father spoke about his inevitable death. We had come to Suursuo because he wanted to show me where I could hunt for food to get our family through the cold winters after he was gone. There would just be mother Outa, little Asla and me, Matti.
I was sad about the cruel nature of the world and wanted to cry. On our way back, we did not say much. It is believed that after death you can take another form, usually that of an animal and I believed that Spot Eye was one of those.

The calf jumps up and rushes to the swamp area with thick bushes on the other side. I am not going to lose my prey and start after it. The thick snow carries the light animal fairly well and it is far ahead of me for a while. Then the crust gives in and the calf does not seem to get much further.

I am reaching my target but cannot get a shot yet. Besides, I do not want it to escape wounded. I pick up my pace as I hear the wolves howling behind me. The thick snow crust is making it difficult for the calf to move and its ankles look bloody. All of a sudden it stops: perhaps it has given up on the escape. As I decide to go for a clean shot and take out my bow, the calf turns its head toward me and looks right at me. Spot Eye! I turn the bow away from it when I see it is the same calf that so trustingly took the grass off my hand.

The wolf pack has reached the swamp and is heading towards Spot Eye and myself. Spot Eye turns and tries to run. I must rescue it before the wolves catch it. Or am I the one being chased? They are getting closer and make a curve when they pass me. I follow the pack leader and take a shot. The wolf falls down. Spot Eye is just reaching the bushes when the pack stops and turns to see who is down. They race to the easy target and soon a dozen wolves are fighting over the meat. When the show is over, only pieces of fur and bones are left. But what will happen to Spot Eye? At least this wolf pack won't harm it for a while and it returns to where it came from.

40. The dead and the living
The Cave of Beasts, 8,000 years ago

- It must be seven years of grief since the day of judgment!

- You're right; and that's why I decided to do a painting on the wall about those horrible incidents.

- These are not part of the good things we want to remember.

- They certainly are not. I'm painting the picture to make us remember what should never happen again. It all started when the headless beast attacked us and ate dozens of our finest fighters. Our weapons were useless against the invincible beast!

- The bloodshed didn't end there. The beast claimed thirty heads for the thirty strikes it had received during the fight.

- We were holding our hands high pleading for our lives. Only three of us were spared from execution. Being the youngest, we were lucky to be standing at the end of the line.

- I see you have painted the deceased greeting us as if they're waiting for a reunion.

- Aren't we all waiting for an eternal life after death? At least that is what they teach us.

- Have our priests been able to explain what led to the unfortunate events?

- Well, our priests are probably looking after their own interests. We might not want to discuss this in public, though, if we want to keep our heads. The thing is, the animals of the desert are also suffering from the worsening conditions. It might be that our apparent prosperity caused their violent outburst. All of this happened because of our endless greed.

- Do you mean that man created this catastrophe with his own actions?

- Unfortunately yes. I don't see an end to this until there is only an ocean of sand as far as the eye can see.

41. Gathering honey
Araña, 8,000 years ago

- So you are planning to climb up the lianas again and fetch honey. Please be careful, I heard last time you had quite a welcome from the bees.

- I'm probably immune to those buzzers now. 20 stings did hurt, but I would do anything for honey. Smoke helps and hopefully the wind won't blow it away.

Having a bag for the honey on his waist, the man starts his slow climb towards the beehive. The beehive is just a few meters away and he can almost reach it. Just as he is putting his hand into the nest, the wild bees start protecting their home furiously. The air is thick with bees that are using their poisonous stings against the intruder. The honey gatherer panics and tries desperately to reach the liana.

He loses his grip and plunges head first to the rocky hill...

42. The Circles of the Sun
Kondoa, 8,000 years ago

- Well isn't that our Sun, portrayed by the strong fingertips of our own ancestors. It is our guide through darkness. Hunters chasing antelopes, more suns, a giraffe with suns on its and a human-like figure who must be our shaman wearing a disguise...

- Our whole life is presented here, all of the past events.

- But what are all those circles that go inside another so evenly?
The last time I was here I didn't notice them, they must be new. How were they made? Lines that are so regular cannot be made by fingertips.

- I got permission to make new suns on top of the old ones, something that's never been seen before!

The painter takes out a device he has developed. It has a thin string with a feather attached to the other end. He fills the feather's hollow end with liquid color. One hand holds the string in the middle of the circles and the other grabs the feather so that the string is tightened.

- Well, what do you know: a measuring device and a writing tool!

- I call this a string compass. It's not finished yet and it would be easier if I were able to draw a whole circle with one motion. Now it's only possible by changing the grip of the hand and drawing the halo in sections.

43. The Elk Boat
Tumlehed, 7,000 years ago

- You look like you're blown away by my painting. Let me explain what you're supposed to see. The theme here is hunting and fishing. Up on the right side there is an elk caught in a net.

When fishermen came to check their nets they faced a peculiar sight: an elk had accidentally caught in the net with the fish.

Further down you see the most commonly caught fish. You are probably wondering about the wave pattern below. They are actually storm waves and not that rare in the waters of the area. Many a careless fisherman has fallen into the abyss because of those waves.

44. The Wedding ceremony
Wadi Tashwinat, 7,000 years ago

Travel log

1/4/2009, Wadi Tashwinat, Acacus

The humid past of Sahara was gradually discovered through the ancient man-made rock art which represented the typical animals of the savannah, such as lions, giraffes and even crocodiles. Nowadays we know Sahara had dry zones even then.

The wadis (valleys) had formed over a period of millions of years and the rainwater went through them quickly. The wadis were partly dried out also in the Stone Age. The riverbed offered shelter for the settlements but did not stop people from moving around by foot. This can be deduced from the fact that there are no pictures of boats.

This painting supposedly represents a wedding ceremony where the bride is getting her hair washed and her wedding dress put on.

It may be that in this picture, like in modern Sahara, grease and oil were used to clean the hair instead of water which might have been low on supply and not to be wasted.

A surprising detail in the picture is the hairstyle on the men. When I was opening my exhibition, The Rocky Chronicles of Sahara on the 18th of January 2013 in the National Museum of Petrozavodsk, Russian researchers told me that the hairstyle in the picture reflects the connection of sexuality to the brain. The hair is shaped like a penis to denote the connection. The researchers were familiar with the subject as there are similar pictures in the rock art of Lake Onega.

45. The deer of Lipci
Montenegro, 7,000 years ago

Travel log
10/23/2013, Lipci, Montenegro

We headed north from the beautiful Bay of Kotor to see the Roman mosaics (200 BCE) in Risan and the rock paintings of Lipci.

The deer paintings are presumably the oldest. These animals with their robust horns resemble the reindeer in the Finnish Lapland. They are dated 7,000 years old.

A swastika-like picture and further down on the right a hunting motif with horses are some of the more recent work on the rock wall.

The location was not easy to find, but the Museum of Risan gave us instructions to reach it from the shoreline. We also got instructions for another route that led through a mountain road but due to the height variation, we decided to disregard it.

46. The Land of the Triangle Heads
Värikallio/Pha Taem, 7,000 ya

Travel log
Värikallio, 9/15/2007

It wasn't a bad idea to go see Värikallio, one of the three biggest rock painting sites in Finland.

Unfortunately, water had run through the rocks and spread the red paint, mixing the pictures together and making the interpretation difficult. There are images of elks, bears and shamans, and also lines and zigzags that are hard to interpret.

Two triangular-headed humans dominate the 10-meter wide, 2.5-meter high wall. Eyes have been drawn on the heads and the other one has a line that resembles a nose. Are these owl heads?

The triangle is a common motif in rock art. Usually, triangles or double-triangles are used to depict human bodies. They are a common sight in the rock art of Sahara, although they appeared fairly late during the period of horses and camels.

A triangle as a human head is rarely seen, but some equivalents have been found. A photo of Pha Taem rock paintings in Thailand is presented here as an example (on the right).

47. Elk riders
Verla, 7,000 years ago

The Swedish historian Olaus Magnus (1490-1557) writes about how elks were commonly used to draw sleds when crossing the Gulf of Bothnia and on the postal routes of Swedish Lapland during the 16th century.

Compared to a horse, an elk was faster and had more stamina. Elks were also able to travel 300 kilometers without food or drink and were easily tamed. Highway bandits often used elks as steeds.

Using elks as steeds was not allowed south of Stockholm on the orders of the king. Because the long-legged animals were so fast, it was feared that traitors might use them to deliver important messages to enemies. Elks were used for riding in the medieval times but could it be that they were already used in the prehistoric period?

We get one answer to the question from a cave painting in Verla where a line of elks is being led by a shaman riding an elk.

In 2009, Finnish media outlet reported that some boys had had the "great" idea of riding a swimming elk. Research on elk farming has been conducted in the national park of Komi Republic.

48. The Bride
Kondoa, 7,000 years ago

- Is this picture about the stealing of the bride?

- Nothing so dramatic this time. I remember when this was painted and it does have an erotic charge in it. In the picture, members of our neighboring tribe are wearing animal masks and they are very excited about their beautiful and well-proportioned gift.

- What do you mean by gift?

- It's a part of an old custom where neighboring tribes exchange gifts which usually mean the brides.

- What about this lot on the left, they're our people aren't they?

- That's right. They are reluctant to give up the fairest maiden of the village and things are heating up.

On the left side, we have a bride from the other tribe offered to us as an exchange. She is a strong woman who will save our bloodline. New blood is needed and this exchange has given us offspring already. I believe the tribes form a solid relationship through this kind of trading. Both groups wish to live in harmony.

- Thank you for the story. Now I'm getting the hang of it. What I suggested about stealing the bride doesn't fit this peaceful image of village life at all.

49. Shepherds on the meadow
Jebel Uweinat, 7,000 years ago

- Is this another painting about a shaman's journey? I thought they were a little different.

- It is about a journey in the physical realm. I took a scenery painting course in the annual Spring Camp for Shamans. The idea was to come up with a more realistic way of depicting our world.

- You seem to be floating in the picture and there are people, but they are quite small!

- Traditionally the subjects that matter the most are pictured bigger. The relations of things reveal the way our world works.

- Maybe this still has a pinch of traditional thinking. The importance of cows is reflected on how big they appear.

- Yet, they don't appear to be big only because they are important to us. Our eyes are built in a way that we see the objects near to us as bigger, whether they happen to be rocks or cows.

- Something isn't right here and I don't see these being used for teaching in the future. But I like what you have done, a picture on a vertical rock wall. It's almost as if you could walk right in!

50. Fire, Water, Earth
UIttovuori, 6,000 years ago

Through the six starry covers,
through the nine heavens,
the spark of fire broke away,
burned the woods and hay.

Is this the end of Kaleva,
to mourn and to keen?
Or perhaps a new beginning,
thought the Son of Kaleva.

The fire makes a fine helper,
on glades the oats will grow,
the cottage will get warm for winter,
sip tea and break a loaf.

In his cabin Väinämöinen
sat with legs astride.
Warming by the log-fire
it was cozy to abide.

51. The Star Laboratory of Lake Onega, 6,000 years ago

- Hey, your sunbeams are acting strange!

- I know, but consider this: The beams of the Sun and the moon illuminate, but only sunlight brings warmth.

- But the beams move straight forward and cast a shadow right behind the object.

- You are on the right track. I shall propose to the council to nominate you as the director of our star laboratory after I'm gone.

- But where will you go? You still hold a flint ably in your hands and the result is sharp.

- I have been thinking of ways to benefit more from the Sun. Right now it stays low and powerless for half a year. If we could gather the rays that diffuse to space, it would improve the heating effect and we wouldn't have to feel cold during the winter... Of course, it could cause some damage, namely everything could burn to ashes...

- Is it possible to change the direction of the beams?

- I call it the Collector. I have been developing the device and tomorrow at noon I'm going to present it. You're welcome to see the show! After all, tomorrow is the vernal equinox and the Sun is at its highest point.
  On the next day, people arrive at the rocks, only to see that the shore is deserted. The wooden shed that acted as a laboratory has collapsed due to a fire. Between the burnt wood lies the charred corpse of the scientist.

52. Elk hunt on skis
Vyg River, 6,000 years ago

- Isn't this a masterpiece, the work of a skilled documenter!

- I tried to picture the whole chain of events as accurate as they told me. The hunt started from the hill on the left. They skied down fast and then they had to climb up a smaller hill. I pictured the climb with frequent ski pole punches. After that, they skied down to Uiku River.

- Is this where the elks were killed? The hard snow crust must have broken under their hooves. Even elks don't move that quickly in conditions like that.

- You're right, the front man skied after the first elk and shot three deadly arrows on it. The big elk in the middle was hit with a spear to its side. The last skier shot the calf with two arrows. It was quite a catch in a matter of minutes.

- Congratulations on the great story. I'd like to hear all the stories of the other pictures as well. There's whaling and everything. But now I have to get back to heating the sauna, we'll continue chatting tomorrow!

53. World born of an egg
Lake Onega, 6,000 years ago

Streaky mother swan,
laid an egg upon a rock.
Hatching it, the golden egg
got smashed into the rocks.
Upper part, the firmament.
lower part, the surface.

Egg yolk became the Sun,
egg whites became the moon,
new stars dappled the sky.
Where the swan swam,
there grew peninsulas,
caves and rushes for the fish.

Oceans rose into the sky,
rained down as lightning,
where it hit merged a ravine,
rivers, ponds, lakes,
birds, fish and snakes.
Bears to woods, deer to swamps.

Pines grew on the hills,
heathland on the moors.
A thousand years went by
little boys were born,
maidens with wide hips.
A people tough and strong.

54. An execution at Vyg River
6,000 years ago

On these court stones,
by the Vyg River,
Fairhair met his death,
this seducer,
sweet talker,
lured a maiden.
Little did she know
about the drudgery to come,
her life as a slave,
an object of pleasure.

Where is Fairhair now?
Struts into the courtyard,
a new maid under his arm.
"Scurry up and bring us drinks!
This here is my new bride!
sleep where the dog sleeps,
this here is my new lass"
"I am not your maid,
from this misery into my mother's arms
I shall return"

"Come back here wench!"
Fairhair took an ax
and after her he went...
By the Vyg River rocks
in a pool of blood
lies the maiden of the west.
Wolverine hears of his daughter,
during his daily chores.
To the black currents
sets out with his son named Hare.

On the rocks the shaggy head
runs with ax in hand.
A careless step and
the killer is on his back.
Out cold, but still alive.
Tied up he is led.
Blood stains the maiden's hair.
The pain of father and brother.
The wail of the slayer,
face down on the boat.

The next Sunday,
death by arrows,
stabs to finish.
Judge is the first to shoot,
hitting the backside.
Brother Hare aims for the nape,
the father cuts the killer's neck.
Further back the maiden young
plunges to the currents,
to join her fair-haired mate.

On this rock I am carving
the events of the afternoon,
the saddest one I remember.
East and West, our whole world.
Hear my highest hope:
live in peace
and our Karelia shall thrive.
Gathering here the remedy.
What herbs will heal darkness and despair?
What herbs will give us wisdom?

55. Palm print on the rock
Astuvansalmi, 6,000 years ago

A feast in Päivölä,
home-brew for the hero.
North Star brightly winks
in the northern Little Dipper.
The woods hear its king roar:
I bear one picture on the wall.

I step into the holy water,
dip my hand in red ocher.
A palm print on the rock,
afterlife can hear our knock,
their present is ours to pass. Our
message here will last.

56. The shaman's misfortune
Haukkavuori, 6,000 years ago

For some reason the deer did not appear by the great Hawk Mountain. The shaman says he will use a hawk, his helper-spirit to find out where the deer are hiding. He can seek advice from the late Great Hunter.

The shaman decides to go see the Great Hunter on other side. The important journey begins from a twenty-meter high cliff and the people have come to send him off.

Something is not right; the hawk that was supposed to lead him has gone astray. The dive of a few seconds becomes a life-long series of pictures. He sees how he was born and how he was raised to become a shaman, a servant of the people.

10...9...8...7...6...5

If the hawk does not show up, this flight might end badly.

4...3...2...1...0!

The hawk flies over the strait and lunges towards its prey. The ice doesn't even crack when the shaman's skull hits it.

57. Mystery of the hunter
Astuvansalmi, 6,000 years ago

Travel log
7/17/2004

I am looking at the picture of the Artemis of Astuvansalmi, but something does not add up. Is this really a painting of a woman hunting?

I used the DStretch-program to investigate the matter and found out that the woman in the picture has a beard!

The Great Hunter in the picture is looking at his prey on the left and is thinking about a second shot to finish the animal off. By instinct, his right hand is reaching for another arrow.

On his right side, hanging from his back there appears to be a quiver. On his right thigh he has tied knives which he uses to drain the prey animal's blood.

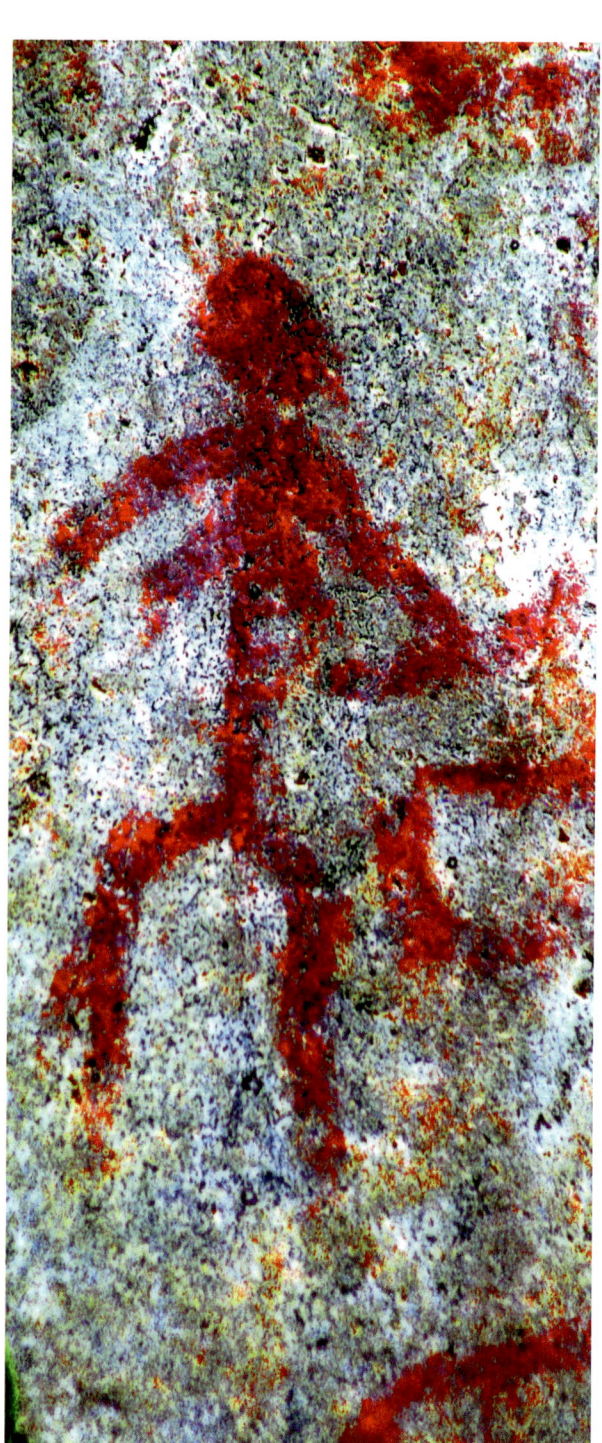

58. Boats for sale
Kannonalus, 6,000 years ago

Is your boat in need for a repair? Maybe it's time to change your old boat to a new one?

Are you looking to catch pike in their spring spawning or wanting to go duck hunting in the fall?

We can get you all types of vessels whether you want to go solo or in a group with up to eight pairs of oars!

Come and check out our selection, the most popular models are available straight away. Let us know what you are looking for and we will deliver your dreamboat in no time!

You can find us downstream just a few strokes of an oar away!

59. The Great Elk
Novoromanovskaya, 6,000 ya

It is very dark, the time of the new moon. The calm surface of the lake only reflects the rays of the Morning Star. The village folk are starting their daily chores. The eldest of the village pokes the fire and moves the water pot closer. He stares eastward behind the mountains with suspicion.

Something is not right, the Sun is supposed to rise soon, but the horizon is getting darker...

- Sound the alarm! The Sun has been stolen!
I just saw it shimmer behind the mountain and now it is gone.

- Men, take your bows and rush up to the cliffs! The Great Elk has stolen the sun again! There is no time to lose, we must get the sun back before the elk takes it underground.

The men of the village are accustomed to acting quickly. The cause is usually wolves and bears stalking on the rocks. A group of archers are already climbing up the rock. The Sun is starting to rise above the mountains and the men disappear behind the rock. The surrounding nature also wonders about the events and the birds are quiet.

People at the village have gathered around a campfire watching the black Sun that is slowly rising from the horizon. At the same time something strange happens: a beam

of light on the edge of the Sun gets stronger and grows into a bright stream of pearls... A glimmer of hope goes through the camp, the Great Elk is losing its grip on the Sun.

- The Sun is saved! Look how it's growing bigger and bigger!

The men run down the cliff accompanied by cheers. The hero who shot an arrow at the elk is being carried on their shoulders.

- Have some tea our brave hero! You got the thief with a well-aimed shot, you mustn't be modest!

- Maybe I hit it or maybe I didn't. The elk went behind the rock and vanished from sight.

60. Shamans of Sagan-Zaba
Baikal, 6,000 years ago

Travel log
8/20/2003
Sagan-Zaba, Baikal

The rock art area of Sagan-Zaba is located on the shore of Lake Baikal about 50 kilometers south of Olho Island. The marble rocks have aged and darkened, making the carvings stand out in their whiteness. The researchers say that the limestone rocks have several caves that have been used for rituals.

There are about 60 carvings of people, deer and swan. There are also pictures of everyday life: hunting scenes, birth and death.

Many of the pictures portraying humans present a horned dancing figure. Even though pictures of shamans are not uncommon in the rock art of Siberia, this type of repeated depiction is rare.

The size of the carvings is 10 to 50 centimeters and they date back to the early Stone Age. Some researchers think they are even younger, up to the bronze period. They base their dating on the technique of the drawings.

61. The enlightened mushroom-head
Altai, 6,000 years ago

- Would you mind telling a novice shaman about mushrooms? How are they collected and used?

- A shaman's mission is to be a mediator between earthly and spiritual matters. You have to have a sensitive mind to do this.

- Which mushrooms should I learn about first?

- My uncle, a noted shaman used to say: As long as it has a red cap with white spots it doesn't matter what kind it is. You shouldn't try other mushrooms. A word of warning is in place; my uncle tried a small amount of a white-capped mushroom and it was so strong that it burned his throat. He said he reached a new level of understanding and didn't even need a helping spirit to fly.

- So he found a great tool for his work.

- At first, yes, but he had to increase the dosage when it didn't work as well anymore. After that he couldn't speak clearly and started to throw up a lot. His mouth would foam and his legs stopped carrying him. For the last few weeks, he stopped eating and was in agony. He had a glorious end in the blazing flames. Here's a word of advice from someone who knows mushrooms: only pick the ones you know!

- What about the use? Are they eaten fresh or do you have to process them somehow?

- Mushroom caps are traditionally dried in the sun to preserve them. The best effects, however, are achieved by consuming the red surface of a fresh cap. The taste is horrible, but you get used to it. You can use honey to make it taste better and to keep it in...

Here: I have tried to picture some of the effects the mushroom gives. My head turns into a cloud that's growing and growing... I rise up into the air and glide above the herds of deer... My head is filled with different ideas and I see through my hands and my skin... My memory expands... At times I'm chasing my thoughts - and at times, my thoughts are chasing me towards something that is hidden... My head shines like a lamp, guiding me towards the truth...

62. The bear's nest
Alta, 6,000 years ago

Travel log

7/4/2008, Alta, the Northern
Norwegian

Here we are at the biggest rock art site
of the Nordic countries. The wooden
sky bridges are well built which is good
because the visitor rates are high and
the bridges are being used a lot. It is a
popular site.

The pictures are painted red which
helps to distinguish and outline the
compositions. Some people are
grateful for this, but it makes the
drawings feel unnatural. Others think
that the red might have been painted
during the original carvings. Do the
colors harm the original drawings? It is
said that the water-based colors now
used are more gentle to the original
drawings than the ones used before.

Some of the originals have been left
untreated. This is good because a rock
art enthusiast does not appreciate
pictures that have been carelessly
painted over the originals. The paint
misses the lines on the carving and
gives a wrong impression.

These drawings represent a bear's nest
and its footprints which lead to the
pictures of the reindeer pens. The
relationship back then between the
people who kept livestock and the
predators is something to think about.

It is probable that bears were a part of the
spiritual world of the people as well as their
daily lives. Humans lived in the nature and
from the nature.

63. The weavers of the net
6,000 years ago   Alta, Vitträsk,Valcamonica

Alta

- Isn't that too loose to be a fish net?

- It's for deer hunting. I'm going to test it at the riverside between the two sturdy trees on the path the deer use. I will set it out tonight. Maybe we will have a live deer in the net by morning. We can build a pen for it and keep it alive by feeding it. In the future, we might have fifty deer and calves growing in the pen.

Vitträsk

- I'm working on a new trap to catch fish better.

- It looks quite small. How is it better than the old one?

- I call it a module net. Weaving a large net is a lot of work but I have created a frame to help quickly produce nets that can be joined together to form a longer net. Those fringes on the sides are for binding the pieces. There is also another improvement, the attachable weights keep the net balanced even through the roughest waves.

Valcamonica

- The pattern of your net looks odd. I doubt that's going to lure any fish. Wouldn't it be easier to weave a net with a more regular pattern?

- It is not so much intended to lure the prey

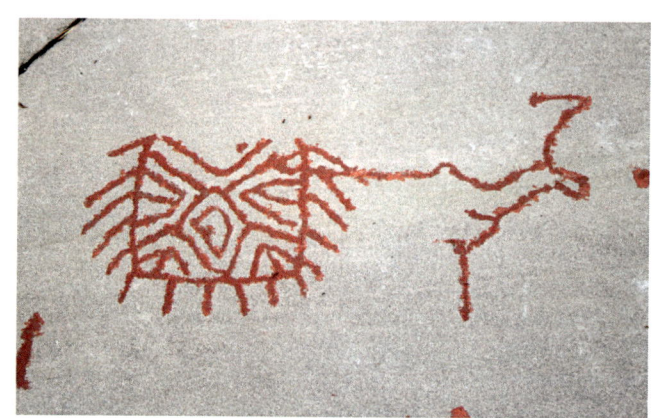

as it is to bluff them. This is not a fish net. The bird hunters complain about losing most of their arrows while hunting the small birds. There are so many birds during the early autumn that if catching them wasn't so difficult they would make a nice addition to our meals. So you see this is a bird net and the pattern resembles tree branches!

64. The Trolls
Pyhävuori, 6,000 years ago

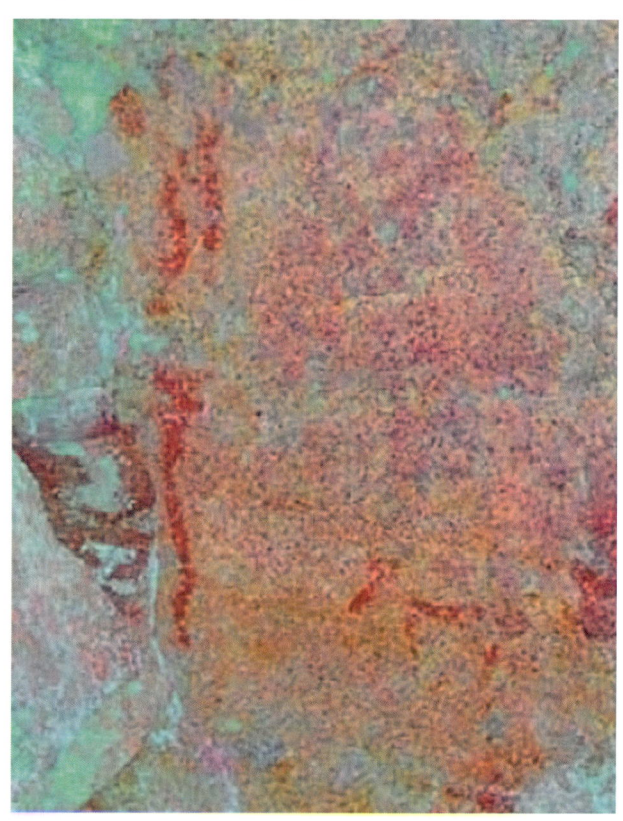

Travel log
7/15/2012, Pyhävuori, Alajärvi

Pyhävuori (Sacred Mountain) is located at the border of Alajärvi and Vimpeli, about 1.4 kilometers from Lappajärvi and a kilometre from road 7421. Its highest point is 148 meters above sea level. The rocky mountain terrain holds many cave-like hollows. A lot of oral tradition is associated with the area of Pyhävuori: it is said that trolls lived in the caves and that the Birkarls sacrificed Sami children on the great boulder called Siankärsäkivi.

The rocks of Pyhävuori have a number of red ocher marks. The experts argue whether the marks are rock paintings or natural hematite runoffs. The latter view seems questionable as the marks form clear images of an elk and the lines of snakes... This piece of art is from the hermitage of Jaakko Reipakka (1855-1932). The photograph has been processed with the DStretch-program. (EL)

The Trolls of Pyhävuori

There is a story about the trolls in Pyhävuori caves. They enter the cave through a round open hole. Many times have the men of the community rolled a large rock in front of the entry but from an unknown reason the rock has been removed every time. None has dared to go very deep down the hole of the mountain trolls. The sauna of the hermit Jaakko Reipakka was in front of the cave.

65. The crocodile devours the Sun
Shiskin, 6,000 years ago

Travel log
8/14/2003, Shishkin, Lena River, Russia

The Shishkin rocks have pictures from several thousands of years, the oldest being from the Paleolithic period up to 15,000 years ago (Okladnikov).

Starting from Lena River, the narrow paths climb up the Shishkin rocks. It is tempting to support one's hand on the rocks that line the climb, but we have been advised not to do so. There are a lot of adders living in the terrain. There is a sign on the side of the road that forbids climbing to the rock art site. We solemnly swear not to touch the drawings and paintings.
The guard of the area gives us a special permit to climb the hill and photograph the rock art.

Obviously only a few obey the restrictions because the art works are damaged by drawn autographs and other intentional harm. When we ask the guard who is responsible for the wrongdoings, he responds:
- It's not the locals but the tourists!

The tourists do not seem to have come from afar because the writings are in the Cyrillic alphabet!

We go and examine the drawings and paintings at sunset and at the break of dawn. Going down the steep hill is especially tricky. At one point, a group of vipers forces us to change direction.

The rock art site of Shishkin has a versatile range of motifs. It is regretful that the appearance and message have been disrupted. Unfortunately, it has been the fate of almost all of the Siberian rock art sites.

Because of the harmful actions of humans, rock art is disappearing from the world, but in Siberia it is done in the most shameful way. Destroying the pictures cannot be accepted!

68. The Nordic walker
Nämforsen, 6,000 years ago

- I see you are out with your dog, but where are your skis?

- Winter has turned into spring and snow has nearly melted from the paths in the woods. I thought I would take a short-cut to the seashore through the rocks but before that I should fetch my bow. A flock of geese were flying towards the riverbed.

- You really are an amusing sight, using only poles and no skis. I think I am going to carve a picture of this!

- Do not judge before you know. I could have taken normal wooden sticks to help me climb but these fit perfectly into my hand, they are firm enough, but not too heavy to carry around. Say, have you finished the picture of the spring bear hunting?

- It is almost finished, just missing the final touch. It would be nice if you brought a couple of geese from your trip. These pictures of elks, bears and boats are getting tiresome. I need a challenge.

- Speaking of boats, you must be aware of our plans to build the biggest boat in the region. It is going to fit twenty rowers and have a double bottom which makes longer journeys safe.

- Of course, I have not missed the construction. Everyone is talking about expeditions to the East and rumors are flying about a land behind the ocean. Supposedly it is not that far away and has untouched forests and all the deer you can hunt.

- The journey can still be dangerous. The weather might change during the boat ride.
It would be great to continue our chat but now I must get on with my trek.

- I will start the picture of you without your skis right away. It will prove to the South that we in the North are not as uncivilized as they think! We are open to new things!

69. The lion man
Twyfelfontein, 6,000 years ago

- Hey, aren't you exaggerating a little! A lion doesn't have five toes and where did you get the idea for that flyswatter tail?

- Hey to yourself! You should also try and look into the spiritual side of things. You do know what the task of a shaman is, right? He has to help the community in daily routines and also have visions about the future. A shaman has to see things from a wider perspective and be able to distance himself.

- So the shamans are tripping for a reason. Here I was thinking they were just doing it for the kicks...

- The lion is the king of the jungle. You have to become a lion to know about its wisdom. The extra toe is strictly strategic.

- And the swatter?

70. The flying elk
Saraakallio, 6,000 years ago

On top of a rock, a stag is looking down towards the strait. At times, it turns its head back with nostrils flaring intensely. Did it smell something interesting on this crisp early spring day? The elk is growing new antlers and right now they look like pegs covered with leather.

I remember that last fall it stood in the same spot. At that time, a young doe was swimming towards the peak where two other stags were waiting. Was that the place to go during the rutting period? Unfortunately, this was not the time for this particular stag standing on the cliff.

I am waiting for inspiration while sitting on a rock with my painting gear. I could paint all the usual stuff but what I would like to paint now is something powerful and at the same time beautiful...

In the middle of my contemplation, a massive stag runs past me. It looks like it is flying when it dodges the sharp edges of the rocks to reach the shoreline. The elk starts to swim when it splashes into the lake.

What could have caused the animal to act that way? I move on to a path that leads to the mountain ridge and see a glimpse of a howling wolf pack disappearing into the spruce forest.

71. Bear hunt on skis
Kanozero, 5,500 years

1 m
Канозеро
Группа Каменный 7 SW
Сцена зимней охоты на медведя

You are looking at what is probably the oldest cartoon-like drawing of bear hunting on skis. The petroglyphs are from group Kamennyi-7 at Lake Kanozero's rock art site.

A man starts to follow bear tracks on skis. After a climb onto a hill, he gets the bear on sight and skies down swiftly. When he reaches the bear, he takes his skis off, takes four steps and hits the bear with his spear...

The story is reminiscent of the elk hunt on skis at Vyg River (Zalavruga).

The petroglyphs of Kanozero became public in 1997. The drawings are located in Lake Kanozero in Kola Peninsula about 30 kilometers north from the White Sea. About

1000 pictures have been found in 18 groups of drawings. The pictures are mainly from the islands of Kamennyi, Elovyi and Gorelyi.

The drawings depict animals (whales, fish, elks and deer), boats, people and different footprints. The meaning of some of the pictures is not known. The drawings and how they were handled brings to mind the rock art of Vyg River, Ponoy River, Alta, Nämforsen and also the rock paintings seen in Finland.

72. Decoration of the cattle
Las Geel, 5,000 years ago

Travel log
3/04/2012
Las Geel, Somaliland

The pictures of the cattle of Las Geel are located 50 kilometers northeast from Hargeisa, the capital of Somaliland. We reached the border from the Ethiopian side. Our travel agency had organized a transport to the border which we then crossed by foot to Somaliland. A taxi driver chewing on khat was waiting to take us to Hargeisa to spend the night. The next day we headed towards Las Geel.

The rock art site of Las Geel was unusual: cows, cows and more cows... Many of the cows were ritually dressed in striped garments. The leaders of the ritual were dressed in the same way as the cows and the paintings also showed dogs, foxes, wolves and a giraffe. The age of the pictures is still a mystery, the estimates range from 3000 to 9000 years.

A French group of archeologists brought the drawings of Las Geel to public awareness at the end of 2002. Several corresponding rock art locations have later been revealed throughout the region.

The day went by quickly while photographing the decorated cattle. Next day we had to return to Ethiopia and continue our journey. (EL)

73. The horns of Aries
Oglahty / Luine, 5,000 years ago

Travel log
9/03/2000
Oglahty

Our trip to Khakassia continues south along the coast of Yenisei River and behind the mountain ridge of Oglahty, about 30 kilometers from Abakan. The ridge offers a magnificent view of Yenisei.

The rock drawings depict animals, people and some abstract patterns, such as the "horns of Aries".
EL

Travel log
10/22/2011
Luine

I came across the same horn motif on my trip to Valcamonica in 2001.

Now ten years later, I could again note the same. The pattern is almost identical to the horns in Oglahty. The only eye-catching differences are the points under the arches which are missing from the Oglahty drawing.
EL

74. Cups and rings
Northumberland, 5,000 years ago

A number of drawings representing cups and rings are found in Northumberland. The age estimates range from 3,000 to 5,800 years old.

For what purpose were they made? Are they connected to a ritual or a holy service? We were establishing a new relationship with nature 4,000 to 6,000 years ago by moving from hunting and foraging to agriculture.

The patterns are represented individually and as groups where the inner rings are connected with a groove.

There are 1,200 separate petroglyphs in Northumberland. The nearby regions of Yorkshire, Cumbria and Durham have similar geometric drawings. It appears to be a northern phenomenon.

In other parts of the world, geometric drawings usually include people, which is why the purpose of the pictures is easier to assess.

75. Basics of elk hunting
Norforsen, 5,000 years ago

- Welcome to the center of the hunter and gatherer culture here at the rapids! The exhibition offers recent information about flora and fauna: you will learn how elks and other animals are hunted, what roots and other plant parts are suitable for consumption, and what berries and mushrooms are edible and safe to gather. Feel free to look at the rock art collections and tour the indoors of the center. Please ask if you have any questions!

A group of under ten-year-olds is chattering while moving from one picture to the next.

- There are big elks and small elks but how come some elks have one or two spots on their behind and some don't have any? Can somebody tell me why?

- My dad says that a girl elk's behind has two holes and a boy elk has a willy like real boys have.

- Well, don't you sound the expert on gender matters! It is important to separate does and stags when it comes to hunting. How many of the elks are girls, and how many of them are boys affect the size of the whole herd.

- But who makes those marks on the elks?

- They are not marked. A skilled hunter can spot the sex of an elk from a distance. These marks in the pictures are here to guide us to the subject. It takes years of practice to identify the sex of the real animals.

76. Builders of Jätinkirkko
Kastelli, 4,700 years ago

- How long do we have to carry these rocks?

- How should I know!

- Who wanted us to do the work?

- It's not about what we want to do, it's what we must do!

- You can ask, can't you?

- Why don't you go and get another rock. Leave the thinking to the wiser. In these days of unemployment, how else could we get seal fat on top of our bread?

77. The Coppersmith
Oukaimeden, 4,000 years ago

Oukaimeden is one of the most important rock art sites in Morocco. It is located 2,600 meters above sea-level and 50 kilometers southeast of Marrakech. There is a popular winter sports center in the slopes of Oukaimeden.

Most of the images are carved 3,500 to 4,300 years ago and date back to the Copper Age and the Bronze Age. The pictures are similar to the pictures in Mont Bego and Valcamonica and they mostly present daggers and other weapons. The first copper items are about 4,300 years old. We know the manufacturing of bronze objects started 4,000 years ago which helps us assess the age of the pictures. The daggers made of copper were probably not meant for practical use. They might have been used for ritual purposes.

Along with the weapons, the collection includes animals, people and anthropomorphic as well as zoomorphic pictures. There is also a lot of geometric patterning.

78. The face of a devil
Qajartalik, 4,000 years ago

- I heard you are working on a picture collection about our ancestors?

- Yes, I want to commemorate them now when we still recollect them.

- Scary-looking bunch! You're not saying we're the offspring of devils? To my knowledge, they were the most loveable people.

- It's a shame you see my pictures that way. They are a bit weather-beaten, I'll give you that, but I didn't want to embellish them. If I wanted to picture them with horns, I would have placed them in the middle of their foreheads.

- Oh, I see! Forgive me for even thinking that about our honorable forefathers. Please don't tell anyone I said that!

- If you must know what these so-called "horns" are, I'll tell you. They don't do this anorak model anymore, but I think in the old days they added tufts to distract seals and walruses. What they wore during the hunt was essential, why not bring it to the carvings of the hunters?

79. Holy Spirit
Horseshoe, 4,000 years ago

The rock art destination of Horseshoe in the national park of Canyonland is located 300 kilometers southeast from Salt Lake City. The paintings and drawings made by Native Americans are estimated to be 4,000 or even 8,000 years old.

Shamanism is an essential part in different Native American cultures and is also present in the carvings in the canyon of Horseshoe: the High Gallery, the Horseshoe Gallery, the Alcove Gallery and the Great Gallery. Near the latter, you can find a footprint of a three-toed dinosaur.

80. Asking the ultimate questions
Coso, 4,000 years ago

The largest North American rock art site is located at the Naval Air Weapons Station in the Mojave Desert in California. There are tens of thousands of drawings in the 250 km2 area and most of them represent bighorn sheep. There is also a number of geometric images and pictures of shamans in the area.

The region has been inhabited for 13,000 years. The drawings are estimated to be 4,000 years old at most.

It is thought that the drawings have something to do with hunting magic. There are other possible explanations, such as shamanism. The picture on the lower right is from the Parrish Gorge and it is connected with an animal funeral and propitiation of the animal spirit. The picture depicts the death of a bighorn sheep with its skull placed on top of a sanctified spear. The motif of dots in a spiral formation might present the sheep's spirit returning to life after which means it can be hunted again.

Similar animal rites have been documented all over the world. One example is the bear rite in Finland.

81. Eyes on the sky
Eter-Köl / Bornholm, 3, 000 ya

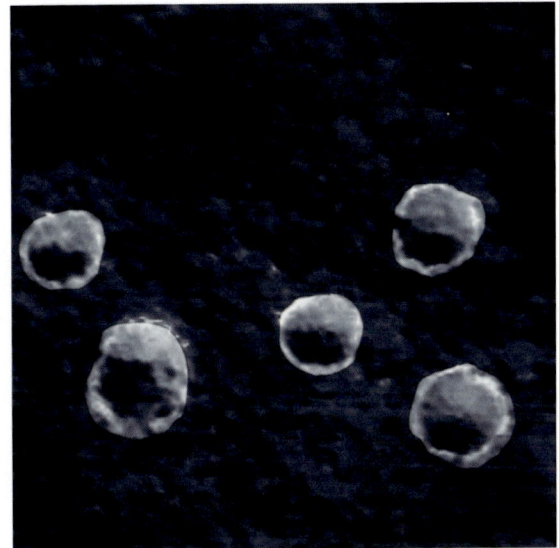

Cassiopeia is a bright five-star formation that is visible throughout the year at the left side of the Big Dipper when viewed from the northern hemisphere. Northern peoples have long been familiar with Cassiopeia. There are mythical stories telling about the "W" or "M" shaped antlers of elks and deer that resemble the star pattern. Cassiopeia was a popular and important subject in rock art during the Stone Age.

The first petroglyph is from the riverside of Ak-Köl in Altay, about 2100 meters above sea level. In this picture that is upside down, the "W" has taken an animal form.

The second petroglyph, probably from the Bronze Age, is from Bornholm's Almegård in northern Rønne.

Cup mark petroglyphs are found throughout the globe, but the meaning of them has remained obscure. Generally the cups are thought to have something to do with agriculture: people made offerings in order to ensure a good harvest.

The cup marks in Sweden have been connected with the Bronze Age. Some pictures are thought to be from the early Stone Age. The cup marks in Finland are from the Iron Age and the cup mark tradition might still have been alive in the Middle Ages.

In many locations, the placing of the cups seem to be connected to star formations. The people were perhaps asking for a good harvest from a cosmic level.

82. Run for your life!
Omadumba, 3,500 years ago

- Is that the tree with the bees?

- Yes and that big crack in the trunk goes up from the bottom to the top. It's probably caused by a lightning strike. We were aware of the bees and this time we had a lot of gatherers to collect the honey. I wasn't too keen on climbing the tree, but I helped the others to go up.

- You had no coverage on your faces and your hands?

- Normally there was no need for protective clothing. If you worked calmly there were no problems!

- A million bees started to defend their hive so something must have gone wrong. Looks like you had to make a run for it.

- There was a swarm of bees flying after the gatherers who were running to the plain towards the river. Once they got there, they dived right in and it took a moment before they could get out. Everyone got stung pretty badly.

- What about you?

- I was alright. I stood beside the tree and watched the show.

83. What would you like to have?
Aspeberget, 3,500 years ago

- I have here a calendar that will help you to tell time!

- A calendar? Just a few holes in a rock!

- It's about the cycle of the moon. There are 28 or 29 days until the next New Moon. If you add one stone into a cup every day, in a month it will be full. After that, you can take the rocks out and start again.

- There is only one problem, how do you stop the kids from doing pranks with the rocks? It's easy to mess up the calculations!

- How is it different from what you do now, drawing lines to a tree? Anyone could mess up that system by adding their own lines...

84. Gods of the rivers
Bižiktig-Haya, 3,200 years ago

- Dear friends! We are gathered here in the river valley to reveal the portraits of our ancestors drawn by our brilliant rock artist. Go ahead, remove the deer skin covering the drawings!

People are holding their breath. They have been waiting for this moment for weeks. They are believed to be the descendants of the Eagle who they now finally get to see. It is time and the deer skin is taken down from the rock wall. A white bird shimmers on the rock surface, its every feather pictured with meticulous detail. They have never seen anything like it.

The people of the Eagle respect their heritage. Everyone has experienced the offering to the bird and a glimpse of the Eagle when it snatches its sacrifice and spreads its wings to plunge off the cliff.

- Look! The supreme spirits of the waters are shielded by the wings of the Eagle: Yenisei and Bižiktig-Haya. You already know them from the masks, the old face images that were made long before us. The masks are from a time when our ancestors arrived at this river valley. Let us give a moment of silence in their honor.

People kneel and turn their faces to the ground. What they do not see is the shimmering white eagle who releases itself from the rock surface and after a curve above the people, picks up the generous offerings.

- Next we have a feast in the honor of the mother Eagle and the spirits of the waters. Please enjoy our show "Gods of the rivers" while you dine.

Hail the spirit of Yenisei! Hail the spirit of Bižiktig-Haya!
Roaring rapids and herds of deer bring us word from the mountain gods.
You quench our thirst, you fill our bellies.
Like pearls in a string the stones glisten in the water.
Above us the soaring mother Eagle.
I bathe in the waves of Bižiktig-Haya.
I enjoy a drop from the stream of life.
Now all is well but what will tomorrow bring?
Speak, spirits of the rivers!

85. The Spiral gate
Himmelstalund, 3,100 years ago

- What a strange line, it looks like a snake that's curled into a ball on a rock.

- Our shaman told me to carve this image into the rock. It didn't turn out the way I imagined. This stone material cracks easily but luckily I was given a bronze spike to grind the worst edges. I still have work to do to make it smooth. It is going to be a gate to the afterlife.

- Come now, who could fit through there?

- Perhaps the journeys of the shamans should be understood to happen in the spirit. You raise your powers next to the picture and get tossed into a swirl that throws you into another world. The travels are not harmless for the shaman, I have seen different kinds of bodily injuries caused by the journeys.

- Sounds like it is a pipeline between two worlds, a time machine of sorts. There are stories of a shaman who went on a journey and to everyone's surprise, ended on top of a mountain on the other side of the river. But who knows if it even was the same person waving from the mountain.

- You shouldn't doubt. With his knowledge, he is irreplaceable to us.

86. God of the ax
Flyhov, 3,000 years ago

- Who is swinging his ax in the picture?

- He is our ax god. It is said that his second wife poisoned him. This happened about 100 years ago.

- A god? Looks more like an ax murderer!

- Indeed, he was a fierce man. His first wife suffered a terrible death and the picture is about the incident. She had a long and golden hair braided down to her waist. Well, her decapitated head was found on the shore of a nearby wetland.

- What reasons were there to commit such an act?

- They say the wife had a lover who she wished would become chief of the village.

Her husband, the chief, found out about her plan and carried out her execution.

Yet, people had great respect for the chief. While the wife who poisoned him was sunk into the swamp, he himself had a glorious end in his ship that was burned on these very rocks. He was the god of the ax!

- The sad events are well put together in the images. When it rains, the hole on the rock takes just enough water to keep the drawing of the head on dry land. I too, dream of being a rock artist!

87. Day conquers night
Högsby, 3,000 years ago

Swans are honking in the morning sky, the Sun is rising. Snakes slither from their pits, crawling all over each other and settle on the rock to catch the warmth of the rising Sun.
It is a sign of spring, day conquers night. Ships on the shore are bathing in sunlight and the dragons on the bows are breathing fire.

The residents of the golden houses on the hill are waking up. The festival is starting and people are racing to the shore wearing their best outfits. Women are wearing jewelry, men are wielding weapons.

A parade on Snake Rock goes past the ships. The Sun keeps rising, dazzling everyone with its light. The parade master gives a sign on his horn. The show begins. A young girl's hair is glistening in the Sun. She does a somersault while the fishermen are displaying their nets. Four men are carrying the morning catch ashore.

The performances go on in the ships and on the shore. The rocks present years of important historical events in the community. The parade continues its slow, reverent walk from one picture to another. So many snakes, how lucky we are! Let us erect a Sun Cross and dance!

88. The white lady or the black man?
Brandberg, 2,700 years ago

The painting of "the White Lady" was found by the German explorer and topographer Reinhard Maack in 1918. In 1929, the French anthropologist Henri Breuil noticed that the drawings were similar to Mediterranean-style and suggested that the picture was made by Caucasian travelers who had visited the location.

Later research acknowledged that the picture of a white woman is, in fact, a picture of a black man! The man is holding a bow and an object that resembles a goblet. It is assumed that the picture was made by the Sani people, also known as the Bushmen. The imagery measures 5.5 x 1.5 meters and is located in Brandberg Mountains at the dry valley of Tsiseb River. "The White Lady" herself measures 30 x 40 centimeters.

The image has been interpreted as representing a hunter engaged in a ritual dance. The hunter has white body paintings that at first led the researchers to assume that the person in the picture was a "white lady". The image may in fact depict a hunting scene since there is a group of oryxes around the hunter.

Unfortunately the picture has lost most of its grandeur. The degradation has been caused by water that has been sprinkled over the painting so that it would be more apparent to visitors.

89. Spring festival at Girl School
Brandberg, 2,700 years ago

The rocky auditorium of the Girl School is situated high up on the hillside of the Tsisab Canyon in Brandberg Mountain. There is a magnificent view to the sun-scorched savannah and the dry and rocky riverbed that leads to the school. On rare occasions it rains heavily and the riverbed is flooded. When this happens the school closes down and the students have free time.

Pretty young girls are gathering their instruments and getting in line. The instruments are played with a musical bow, the sound echoing from the hollow fruit of the calabash tree.

To celebrate spring, the musicians are dressed scantily showing off their body paintings and the nacre ornaments in their hair. The villagers have gathered to see the show and the festivities can begin.

Tomorrow everyone must join in rounding up the cattle to the green pastures up on the mountainside. It is a tough chore because the higher plateau is not reached until twilight. The mountain air is more pleasant, it has more humidity and coolness. It will take months before the autumn rains flourish the land and the villagers are ready to return to the savannah.

90. The illustrator of Halley's Comet
Nadro, 613 BCE

- Why is our rock scribe gazing towards the north? Is something interesting about to happen in the sky?

- There is always something interesting going on up there. The starry canopy is usually quite stable, going slowly around the navel of the Earth that stands still. But now there seems to be a disturbance in the stability and I have been keeping track of its movements. First it looked like it was moving towards us which could lead to the collapsing of our world. I can barely imagine how it might affect the crops. Fortunately, it seems to be moving past us but it has to be marked down on the rock for future reference.

- I, too, have some knowledge of the signs on the sky. A similar thing happened to the stars a few decades ago. My father told me the consequences were ghastly. The sky went dark for weeks and you could only see the Sun through a haze of smoke. Winter took over summer and the crops were destroyed. People went crazy and started to rob one another. Let's hope this time will be different! By the way, how did you plan to depict the view? At this time of the day, it's almost pitch black.

- I'm going to use chalk to mark the stars on the rock and do the real work during daylight. The only problem is that the rock surface is almost full with stories of our history.

- We are clearly at the cutting edge! You are illustrating a present event. For your next challenge, could you depict something from the future? It would be nice to have a peek at what is going to happen when we are not walking this earth anymore but looking down as spirits of the mountain... What will we see then?

91. Time to let go
Frenchman's Gully, 2,500 years ago

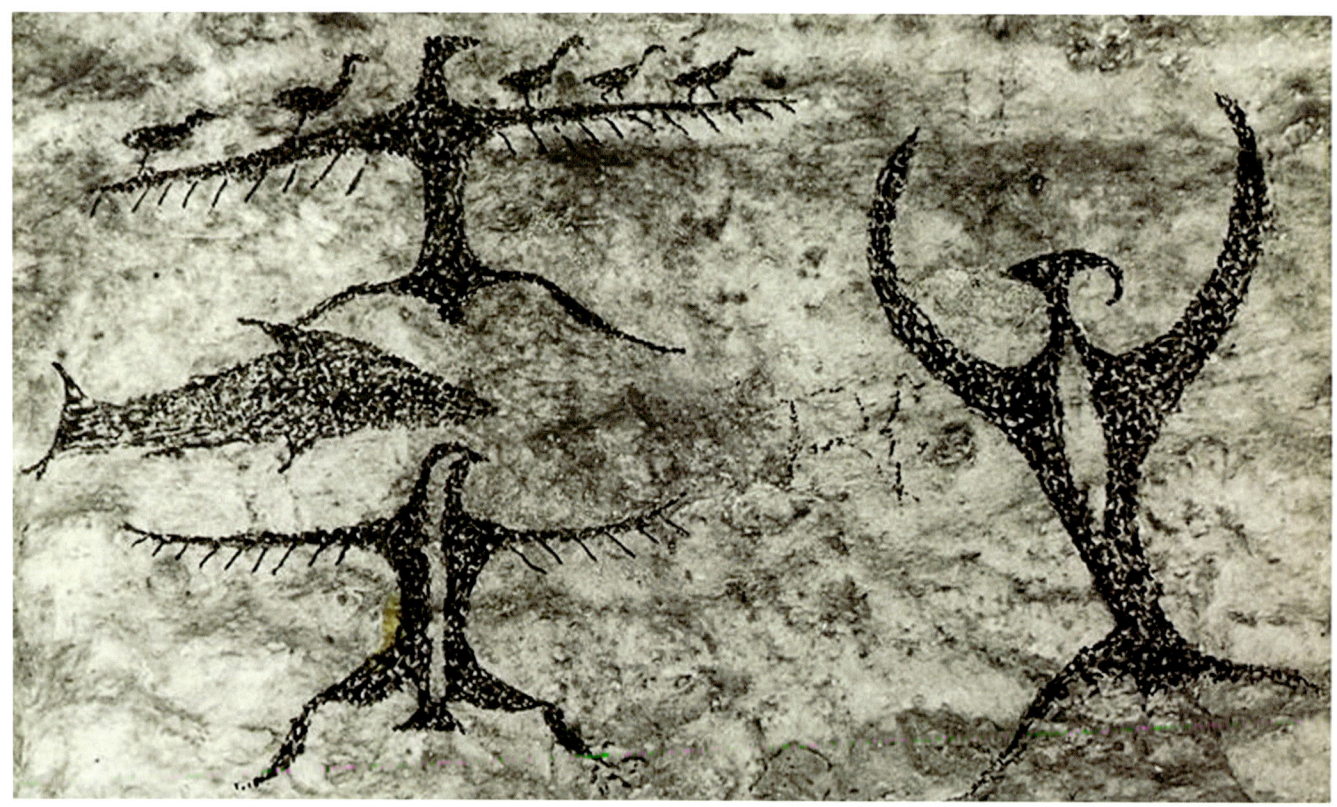

- Hey wait a minute, I have to get my wing feathers in order!

- I doubt that's going to work. Leave the flying to the younger generation. I bet the first gust of wind will throw you against the rocks.

- You might be right. It's hard to give up being a medicine man. It feels like only yesterday I flew the double twist and landed with a perfect forward roll...

- There are plenty of things to do on the ground. It's not all about flying.

- I feel depressed. I think I'm going to take the rest of my medicine, climb up the hill and die. Birds can go ahead and scavenge me. You can throw my bones to the raving rapids, to the mud, to the abyss!

- No way... Why don't you do what the soothsayer does? Start training birds like hunting hawks and homing pigeons to help other medicine men. Let's go talk to him and get you some tips for your new aviary.

92. The first knight of Lombardia
Nadro, 2,500 years ago

- Step down from your steed and lower your spear you mad man! Fight like a real man!

- Are you talking to me? There is no room for loudmouths like you upon this land. I am the mighty Capallarius and this is my squire Posse. The spearmen in the neighboring village were no match for me as you have heard! Keep your mouth shut if you do not wish to share their fate.

- You probably mistook the fence of a house for a group of spearmen and demolished it in the heat of battle. Know this, a group of peasants is on its way to capture you and your squire.

- Out of my way or my noble steed Ronzino will stomp you to the ground! After that, you will be sorry for the things you have said and for the threats you have made. Furthermore, we must gallop, for my lady, sweet Mirabilis is waiting at the mountains. Isn't that right Posse, my brave squire?

- We have met many loudmouths and roughnecks on our journey but all have scampered off like dogs when they have seen us!

- You call that a noble steed? Looks like that hack of a horse's back is about to break. I doubt you will be able to ride it even to the next village.

- Do not speak ill of my horse, it is very short-tempered when it gets angry. The last one to mock it can barely walk with two sticks. Oh, how he wails and groans!

- Your bride is waiting you say? We have heard from a reliable source that your beloved Mirabilis is an ugly witch with a mustache, bearing her fifth child to the men of the village. Best not expect a pleasant rendezvous when and if you get there. But who are we to get in the way of this sorry sight of a knight. These charades of yours will one day probably be played at the theater of fools.

- Come, Posse, our conquest of Lombardia continues! The lovely Mirabilis awaits her hero. I shall compose a serenade. Posse, do you have your lute with you?

93. The face from the past
Minusinsk, 2,500 years ago

- Mister Mask Master! Are all the death masks of the heroes of Sajan ready?

- The masks still have to be burned. This has been the hardest of all my tasks. The corpses started to rot when they were transported in the hot weather. I had to hold a rag over my nose and mouth to be able to stand the stench. The faces of the bodies had also suffered a lot of injuries and some even had their heads cut off. These modern weapons do terrible damage!

- Well, the figure gets its shape from the model. Are there any demands for the mask from the ministration or from the family?

- Sometimes I do have to stretch the truth. Nobody wants to see a noseless hero! It is hard to add features to a person if you are not sure of the shape of their face.

- What is your process of working?

- I'd rather not tell the exact procedures as my livelihood depends on it, but I can tell you the main parts. They are: the creation of the initial mask, using the initial mask to make the final mask and lastly burning the mask. You can make the retouching work to the mask before it is burned.

- I see there is a big pile of finished masks on your shelf. You must have other clients besides the families of war heroes in need of death masks?

- As I told you, you cannot cast a proper mask from an old corpse that has been kept in storage for weeks. It would be best if you took the cast from the person's face before they die. The procedure is quite harmless. First a coat of olive oil flavored with herb spices is spread on the face, then a cool layer of clay on top of it. Sure, you have to wait a while for it to dry out to be able to remove the initial mask unharmed.

- I have a new business idea! Why not expand the mask making business outside the funeral traditions? Every year you could come and take your portrait and collect a book of faces spanning your entire life.

94. Camunian Rose
Sellero, 2,500 years ago

- What a beautiful rosy cross you have drawn!

- Thank you! Nicely symmetrical, isn't it? This is our ancient symbol both in the physical and the mental plane. The soft shapes of nature depict our beautiful valleys between the mountains.

- Then again when we die we leave our useless bodies behind, our spirit leaves our body and with it the shackles of time and space. Gods and spirits hover above us and our mind wanders through valleys and mountains like an eagle. Read the stars for direction!

- Aren't you afraid that someone might steal it from us? Many Northern peoples are heading towards us. They have no sense of beauty. I'm appalled by the idea of some northern technocrat stealing our idea and claiming it his own, probably changing the loops to be angular to fit his own purposes.

- May Jupiter guard us against that fate!

95. The Celts are coming
Naquane, 2,400 years ago

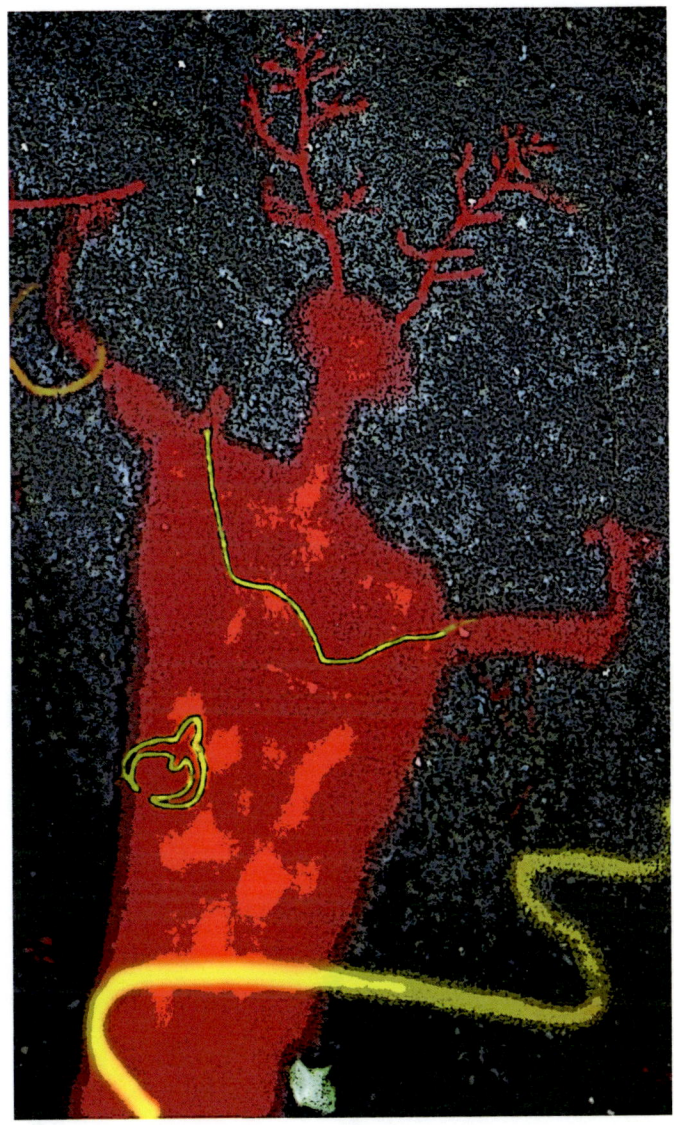

- Are you talking about the Celts? The savage, reeking beings that call themselves Gauls and Celts and whatnot. They think of trees, mountains, the Sun and other things of nature as some sort of gods. They worship for instance this antlered god Cernunnos in their holy groves. They have a blood thirst in them. They don't speak our language so we probably cannot even talk to them, let alone write!

- But our finest troops are being defeated by them which means they must have learned to forge their iron sharper than ours. Our terrified troops flee from the sight of them. They are cruel. Or what do you think of heads cut-off from their enemies and preserved as trophies? This headhunting is probably a way to control the souls of the people. The religious ceremonies of Druids also include human sacrifices. Rest their souls.

- Us Romans have a reason to be concerned about the uncivilized barbarians invading our peaceful villages. The Alps won't protect us from those savages when they decide to head south.

- There is a rumor going on that these barbaric people are already controlling the whole of the northern world and that they intend to conquer Rome here in the Tiber - the mighty Rome that has been ruling the known world for centuries.

96. Troy Town
Hare Island, 2,000 years ago

Travel log
8/16/2011
Hare Island, The White Sea

On our way back from Solovetsky Island, we stopped by Hare Island to see the thirteen mysterious stone mazes also known as Troy Towns. Even though stone labyrinths are common everywhere in the world, these northern mazes have remained a mystery. Why were these arduous projects started to begin with? What is obvious is that the stone mazes were used for rituals but not for burials.

We go around one maze to another in silence. Some of us stay behind while trying to figure out a way to enter and exit a maze. Perhaps the mazes were places where people would meditate and get in touch with their soul.

There are signs that alert people not to destroy the vegetation of the tundra because of its slow development. Warnings are surely in order. an tuhoamasta hitaasti kasvavaa tundrakasvillisuutta. Varoitus on varmaan paikallaan. (EL)

97. Messages of image and sound
Serengeti, 2,000 years ago

The kopjes of Serengeti are small granite rocks dotting the plain. The rocks give a great view of the surrounding terrain and, therefore, are the perfect resting and scouting places for lions.

We approach the Gong Rock with mixed emotions. Is there a blood-thirsty feline prowling behind the boulders? Even though our car is just around the corner there is no room for recklessness. We dare to try out the sounds of the Gong Rock while at the same time glancing at the rocks. The granite boulder is pitted throughout its sides. Apparently these surface variations enable different pitches for the sounds. We use small stones to play the instrument. There doesn't seem to be any Maasai present within hearing distance.

Just over a few hundred meters away there are paintings made by the Maasai. They include wild animals and different kinds of geometric images, such as shields, circles and so on.

On our way back we go past the Gong Rock Kopje only to find a surprise: a pack of elephants has heard our call and has placed itself in front of the Gong Rock. Because we are in a hurry to the Ngorongoro crater, we decide not to repeat our performance.

Travel log
07/24/2011
Gong Rock Kopje, Serengeti

Our tour of the National Park of Serengeti is at its end. We decide to stop by at the Gong Rock Kopje which is a pictograph wall made by the Maasai tribe. The name comes from a granite boulder that the Maasai used to send sound signals in order to gather the community for a meeting.

98. Sibelius and the ancient pictures
Hvitträsk in 1911

The Archeology Committee of The Grand Duchy of Finland in 1911

- Hey, look at this note. Somebody has supposedly found an ancient painting on the face of a rock.

- Does it say who?

- It's signed Sibbelius or something.

- Oh, the composer who is always smoking his cigar. He himself might have composed the whole painting. Hvitträsk... Isn't that a periphery somewhere? Perhaps it was painted by a beginning artist who didn't have the money to purchase canvas...

- Enough of that. Let's meet up at the lobby bar of Hotel Kämp! Sibelius usually hangs out there. We can joke more about the picture then.

The Archeology Committee of The Grand Duchy of Finland in 1915

- Welcome Mr. Europaeus! Now that you are starting here as assistant amanuensis maybe you could organize that box over there. It has dust all over it. Farmers who are harrowing their fields are making a lot of notices about their finds such as stone axes, bronze jewelry and iron utensils. We haven't been able to check everything let alone document them.

The Archeology Committee of The Grand Duchy of Finland in 1917

- I noticed an interesting discovery in Hvitträsk while I was going through the papers from 1911. It was our National Composer Sibelius who had sent the message. Why was the discovery not investigated?

- Sir amanuensis! We simply did not have enough time. There is just too much work.

- I think I might go and look for this rock image. The location is not accurately described, but I should find a net image of sorts... If I'm guessing correctly this might lead to one of our most significant archeological finds.

99. Epilogue: Farewell Karelia!
The year 2030

The nuclear weapon stock in Russia explodes in the Ural. The area of complete destruction has a diameter of 500 kilometers. A Finnish rock art researcher is mapping out the petroglyphs of Besov Nos. The pictures are going under water because of a new dam in Svir River.

Piessa ("devil") now has a hammer, sickle and a star by its side to declare the greatness of Russia. Finland has had to give up all the Southeast parts to Russia. The researcher is taking out tussocks and carrying them to the shore to protect the pictures. He is weary because of radiation sickness and has to work slowly. The situation seems hopeless.

The researcher takes out a bottle of Koskenkorva vodka from his backpack and takes a big sip. The rest of the drops he pours down the heart-shaped crack in Piessa. He sets himself beside Piessa holding in his right hand a one-pound perch which he caught in the morning.

Within seconds, the researcher is soaked with drizzling rain. Further back a dying swan is struggling in a hole, left by a rock boulder that was stolen to the Hermitage.

In the dusk of history
a small primate was born,
learned the skill to mold
our world a better place.
The grip of thumb and index finger
tight enough to pick a rock.

Stone hits stone,
arrowhead and ax of stone.
Ask you may of what and where.
Some become a shaman.
Red ocher, blood and fat.
A picture is worth a thousand words.

Cross the waters by a boat,
ski through the icy fields.
Tamed are the cattle of the woods,
an ox plows the fields of adders.
Stone boards, books and machines,
the instruments of good and evil.

Mulling over upon a stump:
to fish or to hunt?
A thousand times a thousand years
was our life in vain?
Piessa all alone, shedding tears.
In cockroaches the future.

100. A new beginning
After millions of years

Star diary
Sector XZ135, MM208, HY003
15.07.555.473.669

I just landed on the shore of a raging ocean on an unknown exoplanet. There are clear signs of a past civilization. There has also been a nuclear disaster here millions of sidereal years ago. There does not seem to be noticeable radiation in the area.

I am just observing an image presenting intelligent apes. They seem to be decorative, one has a long fringe.

Wait a moment... I am taking cover... Huge meter-high beetles. They are cleaning the mating picture from pine needles and other garbage. An investigator of old civilizations and evolution biology would be useful here.

The creatures are approaching, their front legs are held high... My end has come. Now they are stopping and beginning a sort of chant... Perhaps they see me as their new Messiah landing from the sky...
(WE)

A 100 stories from 31 countries

Vehicles of travel

Lightning Source UK Ltd.
Milton Keynes UK
UKRC02n0254250718
326232UK00009B/42